UNFILTERED AGAIN

A behind-the-scenes look at
healthcare, medicine and mental health

Dr. Patricia A. Farrell, author of
How to Be Your Own Therapist

Book cover photo: uzzi1001@123rf.com

ISBN: 979-8-9986832-1-3

BOOKS by Patricia A. Farrell, Ph.D. (may be purchased on a number of platforms, not limited to Amazon)

Unfiltered: Beneath the noise of our thoughts lies the true narrative of our minds. An honest journey into psychology when the masks finally come off.

How to Be Your Own Therapist: A Step-by-Step Guide to Taking Back Your Life

It's Not All in Your Head: Anxiety, Depression, Mood Swings & Multiple Sclerosis

Work Stress: How You Can Beat It

A Social Security Disability Psychological Claims Handbook

A Social Security Disability Psychological Claims Guidebook for Children's Benefits

The Disability Accessible US Parks in All 50 States: A Comprehensive Guide

Birding in the US NOW!: A birding guide for individuals with disabilities

Sleep, Insomnia, Stress:: What you don't know can hurt you

UNFILTERED: AGAIN

Flash Fiction

Unexpected Short Tales of Surprise

Contents

Introduction

In my second book on these topics, "UNFILTERED AGAIN," I have provided a series of essays that take away the filters that we normally put on what we consider to be sensitive issues in our society. As a psychologist, I try to bring my professional insight to bear on topics that many writers avoid, believing that an honest look is the first step to fundamental understanding.

I've written about disturbing issues such as mass shootings, lying, healthcare failures, commercialized therapy, and institutional power abuse. Each chapter is my effort to illuminate issues that concern everyone but are hardly ever discussed in detail.

I explore domestic abuse, commercialized weight loss, cosmetic dangers, and subtle psychological manipulation. It is possible to present scientific analysis in a way that is easy to understand and, at the same time, observe things with compassion, because I believe that both are necessary to understand these complex issues.

This book is not just my observations; it is my way of encouraging you to look beyond the façade and question the status quo. Whether I am talking about school bullying, the media and body image, or the psychological aspects of aging, I try to offer insights that are helpful.

I wrote "UNFILTERED, AGAIN" for readers who are looking for interesting and thought-provoking ideas about the human condition in the modern world. If you are willing to engage with the unvarnished truth about the social world, I hope you will find this collection both intriguing and stimulating.

Chapter 1: Bloodbath in California Paradise: Missed signs of danger?

G uns and mental health are two issues that hit the headlines too often for anyone's comfort, yet we have another troubled young man, armed to the teeth as it were, mowing down innocent people . It didn't happen the troubled neighborhoods of this nation but in an upscale California town where the beautiful people have homes and send their kids to college.

How many times have you heard someone express shock these shootings happen? How many times have you heard, "But I never thought it could happen here!" "Here" is everywhere human beings are found, and there is safe harbor from a mind obsessed with beliefs of discrimination because they are somehow different. Different, too, can mean almost anything in the mind of a disturbed individual. Stress, life circumstances, personality problems, or any number of other factors can overwhelm a disturbed individual and initiate this destructive darkness.

Can you see it coming? Look at the information coming out regarding a 22-year-old young man in California, Elliot Rodger. Rodger was a multiracial child of divorce, raised in a situation of incredible affluence via his successful film director father, in a new family with a stepmother he wasn't entirely happy living under the same roof. Trips abroad and a luxury car were included in his young life and yet nothing but bitterness, anger and blame were the result. Why? It's not a question that can be easily answered or answered at all.

What did he do, and were there warning signs of the impending fury of horrific shootings and stabbings? Perhaps. The reports from the police in Isla Vista, just outside Santa Barbara, indicate that a rampant shooting spree was planned and executed by Rodger in at least 10 locations. The plan was executed with some care. Three different gun shops were where the gun and ammo purchases were made over a period of months.

It all was put into play, apparently, after he stabbed people to death in his apartment. This act of violence alone illustrates the fury he felt because stabbing anyone to death is an up-close-and-personal requiring strength and extreme ill will. He then took three highly effective guns and 400 rounds of ammunition with him into his BMW and set out for the final kill. There was no anticipation that he would survive, as he admitted his 141-page manifesto.

Who did he want to kill most? Not classmates, professors other personnel at the community college he attended on and off. He wanted shoot women because he believed they tormented him, refused to recognize him as a sexually desirable man, and were worthy of his wrath. One fact that heavily on his mind was that at 22 he was still a virgin and had never kissed a girl. When it was over, the carnage would include seven dead and injured, including the three in his apartment. Among the dead was Rodgers, from, apparently, a self-inflicted head-shot.

Prior to the murderous rampage, Rodger posted a number videos on YouTube in which he clearly stated his bitterness and gave a warning that everyone would pay for their deeds. The language, as I read some of it, sounds like it is straight out of a superhero video game. The theme, obviously, is retribution and doom for those chosen to be plucked from wherever they thought they were safe. Safety was not an option, and he planned to find them wherever they might be hiding. A tone of omniscience was apparent.

Over the years, according to a family spokesperson, Rodger had received outpatient treatment with a number of therapists. His therapist had called the mother because it was evident that something dangerous was about to happen. This is not uncommon and is what any therapist must do to protect the patient and others.

A classic case of intent to murder related in veiled terms to a college therapist is the infamous Tarasoff case. A young man indicated he was having dreams/thoughts of killing TanyaTarasoff when she returned to campus. The slip-ups in communicating with the essential parties resulted in his carrying out his mission, and she was killed.

In this case, the police were asked to make a "welfare check" on Rodger in his home. There the police found a polite, "kind, wonderful human" and seemingly undisturbed young man who said it was all amistake and things would be ending shortly. The ending part does not seem to have been further explored, or, if it was, he convinced police he was fine. Do you recall how convincing Jeffrey Dahmer was when the police asked him about a young man running in the street? He said the young man was a relative who just got upset over something. The police left the young man with Dahmer, and you know the end.

Rodger, in his manifesto, related that the officers were there for only minutes and questioned him primarily regarding his having suicidal thoughts. Were homicidal thoughts discussed? If they had demanded to search his room, Rodger wrote, "that would have ended everything." He feared they might want to make this one move, and he was thankful when they left without it. It is unclear whether the police questioned him about gun purchases.

I know the police were doing a job for which they may not truly be qualified, and it would be unfair to blame them for any slip-ups here. My question would be, why isn't a welfare check done by a qualified mental health professional? I used to work in a mental health center, and I went out on calls like this without any police present. You can often pick up clues that aren't readily apparent to others, and there may be one or two here. We don't know.

Why was Rodger permitted to purchase these guns? Simple. He had no record of being institutionalized or involuntary hospitalization. Either would have raised a red flag. I suppose purchasing 400 rounds of ammo would have raised a red flag for most people who don't have these in their record. You have to wonder, don't you, why anyone would want that much firepower? But there probably are no central records databases of these types of purchases. The NRA, after all, would say it's an infringement of our right to bear arms.

We're now being told Rodger had been diagnosed with Asperger's Syndrome as a child. This autism variant disorder carries with it a great degree of interpersonal difficulty, problems making and keeping friends, and, often, poor judgment. They have difficulty reading social cues and can easily become upset, but violence of this sort would be seen as a rareoccurrence. I've met at least one or two psychiatrists who carried this diagnosis, and they functioned very well in their profession.

Where do we go from here? Again, it's a matter of getting the proper treatment and, perhaps, changing rules regarding gun and ammo purchases. This may not have been as horrific as the Sandy Hook Elementary School shootings, but there are disturbing similarities between the shooters, their diagnosis and the ready availability of powerful weapons of destruction.

I really don't want to hear, "Guns don't kill people. People kill people." Sure, but guns facilitate people killing in numbers too great totally, and it goes on day after day in every part of this country.

Chapter 2: Soaring Medical Fees You Pay Are Set by Whom/What?

Each time anyone goes to any healthcare provider or facility, the appointment, whether for an office visit or some diagnostic test, must be coded on a sheet that lists all of the procedures or patient activities. We generally have no idea who owns these codes, if anyone, and how the fees associated with each code are arrived at by that entity.

Now is the time to pull back the curtain and take a look at some of these things that we have always assumed we didn't need to know. Do we need to know more? I would say we do.

First, let's look at the codes. Where are the codes found on some patient documents? Each time you visit a healthcare provider or facility, you will usually receive an EOB (explanation of benefits). This is how much that code can charge and how much your insurance paid for it, leaving you with how much you have to pay. It depends on your insurance coverage, but there are other concerns here.

Some healthcare providers or facilities will not indicate the correct code for whatever service you receive. This is called, in medical parlance, "upcoding"—sometimes referred to as fraud. Check your procedure codes for accuracy. Yes, all those numbers have a meaning hidden behind them, and you should know what you are being charged for or what you are allegedly being charged for.

I can tell you that, many years ago, after I had had an operation, I reviewed the charges and codes the surgeon submitted and was taken aback. Although it was supposed to be one procedure, the surgeon charged for three different operations and was paid for three operations.

Was that fraud? It wasn't a mistake, and the surgeon was improving her bottom line. It's quite easy for them to do this since patients assume they cannot understand coding, and they also assume that everything is correct.

Not all insurance companies scrupulously check the codes, as in my case. But as to the question of coding, where does this all come from?

Coding History

Systems of medical coding are the conversion of healthcare care services, diagnoses, and procedures into standardized alphanumeric codes. The two primary systems in the United States are the International Classification of Diseases (ICD) and Current Procedural Terminology (CPT). Note on CPT codes: "License to use CPT for any use not authorized herein must be obtained through the AMA, CPT

Intellectual Property Services..." In order to use the codes, someone must apply to the AMA for permission and pay the fee. Does everyone need to use these CPT codes?

CPT codes are not required by law, although it would be imprudent not to do so. Providers are required to use CPT codes when submitting claims to Medicare and Medicaid. Since the majority of health insurance companies follow the same format as Medicare and Medicaid, CPT codes are used by practically every insurance company. Now, the use of CPT codes is copyrighted by the AMA.

The ICD system was first developed in the 1890s as the International List of Causes of Death and has since gone through several revisions. The World Health Organization (WHO) owns and maintains the ICD system globally, with many countries developing their own system adaptations. The United States uses a clinical modification (ICD-10-CM) developed by the National Center for Health Statistics (NCHS), which is a part of the Centers for Disease Control and Prevention (CDC).

As noted, the CPT coding system was established in 1966 and is owned and managed by the American Medical Association (AMA). The AMA is the copyright owner of CPT codes and exercises copyright protection, attracting licensing fees. Healthcare providers must pay to update the codebooks every year to ensure they are up to date with the code changes. How many patients know that the AMA is involved in the fees that they pay and that there is money to be paid to the AMA for the use of these codes?

How Are Fees Determined?

The government plays a significant role in determining the fees for medical services through the Medicare Physician Fee Schedule (PFS). This fee schedule assigns relative value units (RVUs) to each code depending on three major components of the RVUs:

Physician work (time, skill, training)

Practice expenses

Professional liability insurance

These RVUs are then multiplied by a conversion factor (an amount in dollars) to reach the Medicare (in the US) payment amount. The conversion factor is adjusted every year through legislation, and this provides the government with the ability to set the payment rates directly.

Typically, commercial insurers set their fee schedules based on Medicare rates, resulting in a downward flow of effects such that the government's actions regarding Medicare fees affect the entire healthcare payment system.

The RBRVS (Resource-Based Relative Value Scale) Update Committee (RUC), which is comprised primarily of physicians selected by medical specialty societies, makes recommendations to CMS concerning RVU values. CMS does not follow all RUC recommendations but implements about 90 percent of them, meaning that the system is such that the **specialty medical societies' appointees effectively control the fee determination process.**

Accessing the CPT Codes

The copyright that the AMA retains over the CPT codes excludes it from being accessible on their website. However, there are sites that do permit you to do a basic search for specific types of procedures, which are:

00100–01999Anesthesia

95700–95811Sleep Medicine Testing Procedures

10004–69990Surgery

70010–79999Radiology Procedures

80047–89398Pathology and Laboratory Procedures

90281–99607Medicine Services and Procedures

98000–99499Evaluation and Management

0001F-9007FCategory II Codes

0002M-0020MMultianalyte Assay

0042T-0947TCategory III Codes

For each of these code areas, that site also provides an additional source of information regarding what it covers. No, it's not easy to do, but it is important that all patients understand what is being charged by the coding that has been put on your EOB. For example, if you search "anesthesia," specific types of this procedure are outlined as they are for each of the above areas.

What about code 90281, Medicine Services and Procedures? That is also further broken down on this website, and you can search there. For office procedures and other healthcare-related items, the "98000 code Evaluation, and Management" would be where you would search. This website is probably the most useful for patients.

All of this is useful information because patients need to keep track of what their medical records indicate has been provided to them and what has been charged to any insurance as well as what they are being charged. It's as it would be with anything else—you want to keep things correct, and you want to watch your budget. Also, if health records are inaccurate, they can lead to misperceptions of you or your medical status in the future.

As always, let the buyer beware (caveat emptor) because an informed consumer has power and discretion.

Chapter 3: Strength Beyond Years: How Exercise Redefines Aging

Exercise is for everyone, and limiting it to only those under a certain age is irresponsible because it is essential to exercise at any age. We don't need research to tell us this if we look at those walking around us. In a local pharmacy, the woman dispensing medication told me she has a woman who comes in to get her medication, and the woman is 103 years old. According to her pharmacist, she comes alone, walks without a walker, occasionally may have a cane, and is apparently in good health. How did she get there? One truth is evident—regular exercise, and I don't mean the painful kind.

What's more, exercise is just not for your muscles and your strength. I've written on why muscles are involved in mood, and you can go to this article to refresh your memory or read it if you haven't already.

What recent research benefits those over 70? Undoubtedly, we have a great deal more in terms of input in our muscle maintenance than anyone thought when they considered people over 70. The newest research refutes that myth, providing new insights and amazing changes for this group.

But there are specific periods in our lives when certain changes will begin, and with each phase, there will be almost undiscernible changes. However, there are indications that those above 70, who are at greatest risk for instability, balance, problems, muscle weakness, and even bone fractures, require our attention. Previously, adequate work was not directed at the potential maintenance and retrieval of muscle strength in this group, and that is where new, exciting research is coming to the fore.

What Are the Groups?

Sarcopenia is the medical term for muscle loss, and it is a normal aging process that affects all humans, although the rate of onset and the severity of the condition is different among individuals. This slowdown in muscle mass, strength, and function has implications for the quality of life and dependence of the elderly. Muscle loss occurs at different ages and we need to pay attention to enable people to prevent or at least remediate this to some extent.

20s-30s Age Group

In the young adulthood (20s to 30s) age group, muscle mass is at its peak. This age group is likely to have the best muscle strength and function as most people. The body is well equipped to build up and preserve muscle tissue as long as the muscle is used and fed properly. However, even at this young stage, people with sedentary jobs may already experience some muscle atrophy that does not manifest itself clinically. It sets the stage for future deterioration, so appropriate physical activity and diet during these years are a sound investment into future muscle health.

40s Group

Beginning in the 40s, the person begins to show some changes as mentioned above. The literature reviews indicate that muscle mass starts to decline at about 0.5–1% every year after age 30, and the rate increases a little in the 40s. It is also the time when strength reduction is first noticed, especially in muscle fibers, which control power and speed.

The quadriceps, hamstrings, and calf muscles may start to weaken, especially in people with low levels of physical activity. Most people in this age bracket feel the fatigue and reduced physical endurance when engaging in physical activities.

50s Group

More specific features of muscle atrophy can be observed in the 50s. The rate of loss is higher, currently ranging between 1–2% every year. At this time, the hormonal changes worsen the muscle regeneration. To women, menopause reduces the level of estrogen that accelerates muscle loss. Men also have low levels of testosterone that also worsen the muscle tissue.

The abdominal muscles and the lower back muscles, which are the stabilizers, also weaken a lot. Upper body strength, especially in the chest, shoulders, and arms, decreases at a higher rate than before.

60 Group

In the 60s, the loss of muscle is higher, and the following rates are observed: 2–3% per year. The consequences of the changes are seen in everyday life, and the person needs help in performing certain actions. The muscles of the lower limb that include the quadriceps, hamstrings and gluteal muscles also weaken greatly.

Many people in this age group will report having problems with stairs, getting up from a chair, or walking for long distances. The hand grip strength is reduced, which in turn affects the fine motor skills and the ability to handle objects. The sense of balance is also affected because muscle weakness and neurological changes in proprioception occur.

Over 70 Group

Muscle loss is at its highest in adults over 70, with annual losses of 3–5% if no schedule for slowing or reversing this loss is introduced. This accelerated decline has a major effect on the quality of life and independence. This age group has distinct muscle weakness with well-defined patterns of muscle involvement that have important functional implications

The quadriceps, hamstrings and gluteal muscles are the extremity muscles that are affected in a greater degree. This weakness is manifested as:

Difficulty in rising from sitting position

Slow walking

High chances of falling,

Difficulty in climbing stairs. The ankles are also liable to weaken, and this causes the client to have difficulty with walking and increased chances of falling.

Strengthen these muscle groups by including functional exercises that may involve using body weight, resistance bands, or light weights. Of course, any exercise routine in any age group should always be planned with a certified trainer or someone in a rehabilitation facility specifically to address these needs.

Some of the exercises that can be of great help include standing from a chair, slow walks, sitting leg raises, and ankle exercises to build strength. Exercises in water are an excellent way to work on these muscles with minimum impact on the joints.

Balance is trained very effectively by standing exercises that reduce the base of support step by step. The tandem stance is particularly effective — this is when one stands with one foot in front of the other, heel to toe, to begin with, leaning on a sturdy chair or counter. In the event that stability improves, the support can be reduced to fingertip touch, then to no support at all.

The single-leg stance is another basic exercise; start by holding a chair and lift one foot slightly off the floor for 10–15 seconds and then switch to the other side. This exercise directly strengthens the stabilizing muscles around the hips and ankles that are crucial for the prevention of falls.

Weight-shifting exercises are used to develop the dynamic balance. The weight shift is to stand with feet hip-width apart and then slowly shift weight from one foot to the other without moving the feet. Clock reaches expand on this by visualizing standing at the center of a clock face and reaching one foot towards different 'hours' whilst remaining balanced. These movements enhance proprioception, which is the sense of where the different parts of the body are in space, and this sense is often reduced as one gets older.

The good news is that even though you have lost muscle strength, there is still the ability to help your muscles, pull back some of that strength, and renew your ability to move and continue an active lifestyle. As has been noted by several of the articles, water exercises seem to be one of the best, especially for anyone with arthritic conditions. And, don't forget that exercise is intimately associated with mood.

Chapter Four

Chapter 4: Simple Touch Mandates a Significant Place in Health Fostering

O nce, on a trip with a friend to Mexico, she became ill as we
were in a small airport waiting room, seated on benches against
the wall. As we sat there, a middle-aged Mexican couple came over
to sit beside us, and as they did, the woman began moving closer to
my friend. She moved so close that their arms and shoulders were
touching, and the two of us, being Americans, wondered if something
criminal would happen.

The man, sensing our concern, turned and said with a smile, "My
wife sees your friend isn't well and is sitting with her to give her

strength." I hadn't thought much about it, but recent research is pointing to the power of human touch and how it is vital that we incorporate it into not simply our lives but even our healthcare. I don't know if there is a psychic component, such as the Mexican woman sitting next to my friend, but that has yet to be explored, and perhaps it will also offer new insights.

The pandemic brought attention to the idea of touch, and we need a deeper understanding of the ways in which physical touch, and the absence of it when we withdraw socially, can impact our psychological and physiological health.

From aiding development and growth to buffering against anxiety and stress, the most common touch interventions—like kangaroo care for newborns or massage for adults—have a broad range of mental and physical health benefits that persist throughout the lifespan of both animals and humans.

Although there is a great deal of evidence in the literature supporting the benefits of touch, there is also variation in the studied cohorts, the type and duration of applied touch, the measured health outcomes, the type of person applying the touch (e.g., a partner versus a stranger), and the outcomes, such as a one-time hug versus repeated 60-minute massages.

During the pandemic, people were anxious about breathing and physical touch, which caused them to withdraw socially and experience emotional pain. It provided a brilliant illustration of our need for touch. Some people may not get the non-sexual physical touch they need, which is known as tactile deprivation.

According to studies, physical touch positively affects health at all life stages, including reducing anxiety and strengthening emotional bonds. Isolated people can find comfort in self-care, pets, or soft touch. But as individuals, we still rely heavily on the desire for physical touch and human connection to thrive. One graphic illustration that shows how lack of human touch is important for the maintenance of life and development in infants was the research of Rene Spitz after World War II in orphanages.

The children were provided with everything that they needed in terms of food, clothing, and medical care, but the one thing that was not given was human touch. The result was that the children developed poorly and failed to thrive (aka hospitalism and anaclitic depression), and some died within their first three years.

Another important series of research experiments was carried out by Harry Harlow with rhesus monkeys and lack of attachment for infant monkeys. Considered both controversial and inhumane, it nevertheless supported the idea of tactile comfort being necessary for the young.

No one has to tell animals about the need for touch, and you can readily see it if you watch kittens together who were sleeping or, as I've recently seen on the Internet, dogs and cats slobbering together. I've even seen a hen who had been used to hatch duck eggs lovingly care for her ducks and try to cover them beneath her at night as they all slept. It was genuinely touching.

Chapter Five

Chapter 5: "Lemonading" May Help Us Cope with Adversity in Our Lives

A dults dismiss play because they are "adults" and, therefore, play or playfulness is not something adults engage in, correct? Wrong. New research and returning to a prior orientation to life are now seen as readily available means to help us deal with difficult times.

The American Psychological Association reports that persistent emotional or mental strain poses a serious threat to American citizens' well-being. Long-term effects of chronic stress are associated with a wide range of health issues, including cardiovascular disease, diabetes, depression, and anxiety.

Stress levels and the number of people diagnosed with mental illness can rise due to factors such as the pandemic, economic uncertainties, and societal difficulties. The question is quite simple: Do people who are playful see, approach, and react to their surroundings and life events in a different way than less playful people?

Some people think that being playful can change how people see or rethink situations, but this generally accepted idea lacks both theoretical detail and empirical validation. Research looked at fun as a way of looking at things and how it might change thinking, feeling, and acting in a disruptive pandemic setting.

Instead of "rose-colored glasses," playfulness works like a "color spotlight," selectively affecting people by "lemonading"—imagining and following positive possibilities to create valuable and enjoyable experiences while staying realistic about problems. This gives us a complete picture of how playful (re)framing works, showing that it mainly involves goal-oriented, thoughtful, and behavioral redirecting. It's how humor can be used as a resilience factor.

A major study looked at how some individuals coped and retained their health through the COVID-19 epidemic. The Adult Playfulness Trait Scale levels of playfulness. Playful people identified risks and benefits similarly but were more optimistic, creative, and enjoyed tasks more.

Those with a playful zest for life are as grounded in reality as everyone else when it comes to the dangers and difficulties posed by COVID-19. What sets them apart, though, is their talent for "lemonading"—finding "the good in any given situation and making the most of it. It is also essential to play with people who make you laugh and do things that make you happy and curious. And this also applies to work situations.

Playfulness at work has been linked to several results, such as new ways of doing things or personal goals. Researchers looked at how playfulness in adults is linked to the ways people deal with stress at work and whether these ways of dealing with stress help to transfer the expected link between playfulness and life happiness among employees. It does.

Several excellent outcomes have been associated with adult playfulness, according to research. These include increased contentment with life and relationships, improved emotional regulation, higher test scores, a preference for intrinsic objectives at work (i.e., a desire for challenges), and creative problem-solving. When we look at what can result from maintaining an adult-oriented view of playfulness, it is truly impressive.

Ways to Return to Playfulness

One session introduces "Battlement," a technique to slow down thinking and enhance experiences. The instructor emphasizes the importance of relaxing the body to enter this state. Participants are guided through warm-up exercises and encouraged to focus on the back of their heads. A mantra, "I don't know what I'm doing, but it's okay," is repeated while exploring an object and selecting a clown outfit for a photo. Who dresses like a clown? Children do, and that's what it's all about—returning to those fun-filled activities of yore.

Note of Infinity is an associated game that aims to excite the player. A low-pitched note is made in the belly, then slid up to the top of your vocal range. Imagine it bursting through your head and hovering there as you wave your hands in front of you. You feel silly? That's the point because it pulls you out of your usual self and into a sense of playful silliness—exactly what you need. While these exercises may not be suited to what you would like to do in terms of playfulness, there are some simple things you can do.

Simple "rules" to apply for yourself and playfulness include:

1. Taking part in pursuits that make us happy and curious.

2. Being receptive to new information and trying different approaches to old tasks is an example of this.

3. Facilitating chances for impromptu, unplanned investigation.

4. Being in the company of humorous, game-changing individuals.

5. Laughing and enjoying oneself when it is suitable.

No, it's not about silliness or being a Pollyanna; it's about life and mental health. We can do things, even in the worst of times, to help ourselves remain grounded and reasonably happy. Don't dismiss it. Give it a try.

Chapter 6: Salmon Is Taking Center Stage in Kids' Personality Disorders

C onsiderations of diet, as they relate to mental health psychological issues, have been gaining traction in professional publi-
cations —and with good reason. A hefty number of articles in the past
decade point toward serious consideration of healthcare professionals
writing prescriptions for specific foods or diets. And it's not simply
about how gut health plays animportant role in mental health; now,
research is directed toward personality formation.

A seeming relationship appeared to exist between salmon and
the incidence of a specific mental health disorder. The research on

omega-3 indicated it could lower schizotypy because people who ate more fish when they were 3 to 5 years old had lower rates of personality disorder when they were 23 years old. New research has tested idea.

A community group of 290 11–12-year-olds who met thecriteria for conduct disorder, oppositional defiant disorder, or aggression scores on a standard test were included in the intention-to-treat, single-blind study. Three groups were entered into the study: omega-3 alone, CBT alone, and omega-3 and CBT together. Schizotypy was down 25.7% in theomega-3-alone group and 36.6% in the omega-3-plus-CBT group three months treatment.

Compared to the CBT group 9 months after treatment, theinterpersonal schizotypy factor showed stronger effects in both omega-3 groups. Reductions in schizotypy were much stronger in people who ate a lot of nutrients. The results have indications for benefit not simply to patients, but to society in general.

The high costs these behaviors have for society make ways to stop them important if cost is the sole purpose of such research. I tend to dispute a dollars-and-cents approach and prefer the benefit shown the patients.

One type of intervention is adding nutrients to the food. Research shows a link between insufficient nutrients and acting aggressively antisocially. For instance, not getting enough food when you are 3 years has been linked to acting aggressively and unsocially when you are 8, 11, and 17 years old. Also, randomized controlled trials (RCTs) have shown that multivitamins and mineral supplements can help lower antisocial behavior.

Children not getting enough nutritional food are more likely to have problems with their brains and thinking, which can lead to problems that appear in public throughout childhood and youth. The results that cutting malnutrition in children may help lower antisocial and behavior later on. We know the need for specific nutrients for proper development at an early age, yet nutrition has received insufficient attention.

Many studies have been done over the years on the biological and social factors that make kids more likely to be aggressive. Still, surprisingly, little is known about how poor nutrition can lead to aggressive behavior in kids. It is not often that a nutrition shortage is looked at in terms of externalizing behavior. Still, many studies have shown that additives, hypoglycemia, and, more recently, cholesterol can change how people act. Why salmon and omega-3? How does it work?

Getting more omega-3 may help make up for the structural functional problems seen in people who are aggressive and antisocial. This is because omega-3 helps control the activity of membrane enzymes, neurons from cell death, encourages neurite outgrowth, and improves functioning and dendritic branching. When viewed in these terms, salmon and omega-3 seem like wonder drugs you can easily buy in the fish department of themarket.

If most research points toward these supplements or salmon, one major problem remains even in the face of research singling out supplements and salmon in particular. What is it? Finance plays a major role household incomes; supplements and salmon can be expensive, ergo inaccessible, items to add to any shopping list.

Should local groups or the government begin to provide thesupplements (we know they won't give out fish vouchers) to help kids in terms of brain development and functioning? But the case must be viewed in the face of how violence, either proactive or reactive, adds to the local budgets, instills fear in the community, and may relegate young people to lives of despair or imprisonment. What is cheaper, a bottle of supplements maintaining someone in a prison cell for years? It's patently clear which is preferred.

The time for dietary medicine would seem to have come, and we have to wonder why it's not being emphasized more.

Chapter Seven

Chapter 7: Do Carrots Scream?

"*H*ow do you know that carrots don't scream when you pull them out of the ground?" The student in the biology lecture hall was now the object of disbelieving looks, shakes of the head, and twirling of fingers indicating she must be crazy.

The professor was no less dumbfounded as he stared in her direction. Words did not come to him quickly, and he fumbled for a response. What could he say?

He responded that, of course, vegetables did not have feelings, did not scream, as she indicated, and we should dismiss the subject entirely. After all, we were talking about simple, one-celled plants and their cytoplasm, not carrots, not vegetables of any type. If we had been talking about vegetables, would he have had a better response?

The professor wheeled on his heel, muttering to himself, and returned to sketching the outline of the one-celled plant on the blackboard. All of us, feeling she must be mortified, bent our heads down and turned our attention to our notebooks. We focused on our sketching as if our lives were at stake.

The young woman was left alone in her defense of vegetables, specifically carrots. Carrots would have to wait for a defender more expert than a college freshman. And that day has come many decades later.

Plants "Yell" for Help

Plant sentience was considered pseudoscience when it was proposed in 1973 in "*The Secret Life of Plants*." The book relates a remarkable experience with a plant.

Teaching a course on lie detectors, an impulse, more a joke than anything else, prompted Cleve Backster to hook up a plant to the lie detector. The result was a change in the readings when he watered the plant. It was so astounding; he was prompted to try another experiment.

The idea of setting fire to the leaf to which the electrodes were attached crossed Backster's mind. Just as he was about to grab a match, the graph's tracing pattern surged skyward, as if reacting to the threat perception. In those brief ten minutes, Backster had a life-altering epiphany: plants could sense and respond to our emotions. This groundbreaking concept would go on to be known as "The Backster Effect."

How could a plant know what he was preparing to do? It was preposterous, and the idea of plant communication even more so. But the idea did not die.

Peter Tompkins and Christopher Bird, the book's authors, took up the exploration of the work with plant sentience. The work and their writing were criticized and viewed as little more than pseudoscience. Their proposal, however, was based on research by scientists (George Washington Carver, for one). They had suggested a state of plant life unheard of before and viewed as something belonging in the realm of fairies.

Plants Can Learn and Have Innate Abilities

New research suggests that, if we listen to plants, they do communicate with each other and engage in a type of "talk" as well as protective actions. How can a plant protect itself? An example will suffice.

When voracious caterpillars attack corn seedlings, the plants emit a volatile compound that attracts the caterpillars' enemy, wasps—calling for help? An exciting proposition, but is it under the control of the plant? The answer is yes because this same compound is not found when a plant is mechanically damaged, only when the bug is present and eating away.

How could a plant "know" to do that, and what help would come, especially since these were seedlings without experience? Perhaps we have fooled ourselves by refusing to consider plant life in its whole as no more than simple tropisms.

What innate abilities might plants have? According to research by Dr. Monica Gagliano, plants can learn by experience. In one experiment with a Mimosa pudica, a plant with leaf sensitivity, she dropped potted plants onto foam, and their leaves closed in the expected reaction.

But, after a few trials, they did not close. Gagliano asserts this is because they "knew" the dropping wasn't a threat. To ensure that they could still close their leaves if in danger, she shook the plants; they closed their leaves. Sentience or wishful thinking?

Plant Altruism, Vision, and Math Ability Is Insinuated

Plants, according to several studies, react in a relationship whether or not they are "kin" to other plants in the area. In this regard, they may not allocate resources to their leaves and, instead, increase their stems and branches. This, the researchers believe, is a type of cooperation and altruism in allowing other plants needed access to sunlight.

The mighty Douglas fir may also "exhibit a kind of altruism, using extensive underground fungal networks to share water and nutrients with other plants based on need. This sharing extends to the trees' own seedlings and even to members of other species." Mosses, similarly, engage in helping to nurture other plants within their area.

More than generous, plants can ensure adequate resources for themselves to last through the night. In this, they perform "mental" calculations to measure the amount of starch in their leaves and estimate when the dawn will come so that they can sustain themselves until sunrise. At daybreak, 95% of their resources have been depleted. But they survived the night.

Charles Darwin, in his 1880 book entitled *The Power of Movement in Plants*, opened a new field. In the book, he indicated that plants have the ability not only to move away from obstacles and toward water but also to direct movements of adjoining plant parts. In effect, he was saying that plant root tips are similar to "the brain of one of the lower animals."

Darwin also proposed that there was an electrical signaling system as well as more systems to be explored in future research. Stefano Mancuso, a researcher, also believes that plants have more in terms of abilities than we have ever imagined. He has formed the Society for Plant Neurobiology and believes that plants may "see" by their photoreceptors, which can pick up different wavelengths of colors.

New research is indicating that mushrooms and other fungi do have a form of communication. According to the study, fungi might even use "words" to form "sentences" to communicate with neighbors. The communication was picked up by studying electrical spiking activity in certain oyster fungi. Analogous to nerve networks in animals and humans, the spiking is found in other invertebrates and may be facilitated via specific chemicals.

A recent study with a specific type of fungi shows, according to the researchers, that despite having no central nervous system, they have a memory. There has been a recent uptick in research into the possibility of cognitive abilities in non-brain-containing creatures, including learning, decision-making, problem-solving, and anticipating.

Advancements in this area of study may lead to fresh concepts for bio-based computer systems and a deeper comprehension of fundamental scientific issues, including the roles played by biotic ecosystems and the evolution of cognitive systems in different species. Fungi are at the forefront of the ongoing quest to discover intelligent life beyond animals.

Chapter 8: Fairy Tales Shock and May Deceive—Are They Still Relevant?

C hildren, we are told, should be protected from things that would be inappropriate or frightening for them, and yet we read them, often at bedtime, as fairytales. Adults with children also had classic fairy tales read to them. They want to pass this on to their children, believing that these tales that weave fantasies and have magic for little minds will also bring a sense of morality, empathy, and happiness to the children. Nothing could be further from the truth because the original fairy tales are grim, often grizzly stories embodying the worst human behavior. Try to get a copy of the original Italian Sleeping Beauty if you want to understand how much the story has changed. What do I mean?

For instance, let's consider Jack and the Beanstalk. We believe Jack is a loving child who wants to do whatever he can for his poor mother and sets out to sell whatever he can, which is the family cow. What does Jack get for the cow? A couple of beans, and that sounds like Jack has been scammed.

But Jack, in his optimistic persistence, lets the beans grow (reality is put on hold here because beanstalks don't grow overnight) into a giant beanstalk that Jack naively climbs to steal from the giant who lives there. Do we wish to teach our children how to be better thieves or how to have empathy for poor families? Jack and the Beanstalk is only one story, and it's not the worst.

What about the Little Red Riding Hood, who goes with her basket of goodies to visit her grandmother's house and is stopped by a wolf? It's a pretty grim tale that includes deception by the wolf, the wolf swallowing the grandmother and assuming her place, and, finally, the hero, in the form of a woodsman, coming to save the children from the wolf. Of course, how he saves the grandmother can be unnerving, and perhaps that ending should have been changed.

Hansel and Gretel are even worse when their parents (the step-mother is the instigator here) abandon them in the woods, and a wicked old woman puts Hansel in a cage to fatten him up for eating. Why were they abandoned? Because of the family's financial situation, the husband gave in to her request to remove his children from his previous wife. It's not a pleasant tale to tell children; they might fear being abandoned and left to survive in a forest of evil old women.

There are, of course, lots of different ways to look at fairy tales. Still, it's fun to look at the clear and not-so-clear lessons that these old stories teach kids. Fairytales were even the topic of a famous psychologist, Bruno Bettelheim, who wrote "The Uses of Enchantment," a detailed dissection of fairytales and their underlying messages to children.

These days, bedtime stories can teach morals and useful life lessons, while many old fairy tales have scary or violent themes. These are some good ideas and lessons that children can learn from modern children's books:

1. **Understanding and kindness**: Stories can teach children the importance of caring about others and understanding how they feel and what their lives are like compared to the child's life.

2. **Children can learn to accept and value people** from different backgrounds through stories worldwide where cultural differences are outlined, and belief systems vary. These stories can also help them appreciate how unique each person is and value that, too. In the US, the native peoples have stories that children should read to help them realize how we are connected to nature and must protect it.

3. **Strength and determination**: Adults, whether in fairytales or life, are children's first teachers. They can learn to be strong by modeling the behavior of adults and those who don't give up when things get tough. The thread of persistence is clear in many fairytales.

4. **Being honest and doing the right thing**: Stories can show how important it is to always do the right thing, even when it's hard. Sometimes, it's hardest when the right thing may present hardships for a child. Who shares their lunch with another child who has none?

5. **Creativity and imagination**: The wonder in these tales is that anything is possible—trees can talk, carpets can fly, and people have magical powers. Reading stories that interest kids can help them

develop new ways to complete tasks and encourage them to problem-solve.

6. **Eco-friendly**: Stories teach kids how important it is to look after the Earth and all its living things. Even the tiniest things have a purpose and aid us in our lives. It teaches them to honor life in all its forms. Are their stories about how little insects or worms enrich our lives? Worms in the earth are essential to keeping the ground healthy for plants.

7. **Giving back to the community**: Stories can show how a family or group of friends can work together to help each other. How community gardens may be places of wonder and connection is another theme.

8. **Self-love and confidence**: Kids can learn to be as sure of themselves as characters who love and accept their flaws. They can also learn to use questioning when appropriate.

9. **Working together**: Stories can show why working together is beneficial and the feeling of accomplishment that comes from teamwork.

Children's bedtime stories may contain tales of wonder and hope, resilience and goodness, and that's probably the element that made the Harry Potter series so successful. These tales have the power to unleash children's creativity and mold their perceptions of what the future holds when goodness prevails in the face of adversity.

I recall being on a plane, and when I looked to the adjacent aisle, an older man was engrossed in reading one of the Harry Potter books. Yes, the books, written by a woman who had been on welfare in the UK, had something for kids and adults. Now, she's a billionaire.

Truly, these are teaching stories for the world's children to face in the future, and preparing them may be as simple as picking an appropriate bedtime book to read as they make their way into a safe and comforting slumber.

Chapter Nine

Chapter 9: Computers Can Understand Our Emotions Now?

B ody language is one area where social scientists believe they have access via behavioral indicators to someone's interior life, motivation, or emotions. The research first began with Ray Birdwhistell in 1952 and continues to this day. Birdwhistell coined the term "kinesics." It means "facial expression, gestures, posture, and gait, as well as visible arm and body movements." He believed words carried only 30 to 35 percent of the social meaning of a conversation or an interaction. But now there's a new fillip in technology, which is not without its concerns and flaws.

Based on commonly held beliefs, people can easily determine someone's emotional state by observing facial movements, also called emotional expressions or facial expressions. This assumption is used to make decisions about the law, policies, national security, and education.

The assumption also affects how psychiatric illnesses are diagnosed and treated. Finally, it affects how people interact with each other, and research in science areas like computer vision, neuroscience, and artificial intelligence is probing the depths of behavioral delineators of internal aspects of life.

I recall a young man telling me he went for a disability psychiatric evaluation, and he walked into the room with a smile on his face. The psychiatrist who was going to conduct the consultation did not treat it well. Without notice, the psychiatrist asked, in a very cold, angry tone, "Why are you smiling?" We have to wonder who needed the evaluation.

How Does AI Do It?

With the use of face recognition software, large language models (LLMs) can deduce how a person is feeling just by looking at their face. Subtle shifts in the facial muscles that support our lips reveal our true feelings when we experience joy, sorrow, rage, or surprise. Emotions manifest as changes such as widened eyes, tilted lips, or elevated eyebrows.

Of course, anyone who can limit their facial expressions and keep it rather bland may believe that they can overcome AI's ability to sense their emotions. But one thing they may not do is to control the size of the pupils in their eyes, which react to emotion, depression being one of them. I have not seen this specifically explained in the AI research that I have examined.

AI systems can locate and store these characteristics because they use sophisticated algorithms with cameras. By comparing the patterns it detects on the face to a database of known expressions, artificial intelligence may deduce the emotion someone is expressing.

For example, the AI may interpret the expression as happiness if it detects crinkled eyes and a curled mouth. The AI's ability to interpret emotions from facial expressions improves as more training data is collected.

This technology has numerous applications, including enhancing user experiences and providing mental health assistance. However, emotions are nuanced and can manifest in various ways, and facial expressions can vary greatly among cultures.

We cannot assume that all cultures are the same. In fact, sometimes people have experienced extremely taxing emotional situations, yet their facial expressions have not responded to them. Employing AI face recognition in conjunction with other methods is recommended to compile a more comprehensive understanding of people's emotions.

Not many angry people frown in real life. In the West, people scowl about 35% of the time, which is more than just chance, but not enough to make it a uniform way to show anger. About 65% of the time, they move their faces in ways that mean something else. They might wrinkle their brows or pout. Their eyes might tear up. They might truly enjoy themselves. They could just sit there and plan how to kill their victim.

Mostly, when Westerners frown, they're not mad. Therefore, training artificial intelligence on facial recognition can fail because it does not have training on various cultures and people's responses in those cultures. Are AI scientists addressing this problem? They have realized this and will continue improving their programming, but it's an uphill battle.

Researchers in the field of emotion still believe that people worldwide reliably show and understand certain emotions through specific patterns of facial movements. This is true even though more and more scientists are realizing that people's anger, sadness, happiness, and other emotions appear in a wider range of facial expressions.

People have held this view for a long time, and it guides more than just science. People's understanding of emotions changes because of it, which affects schooling, clinical practice, and business uses. It affects almost every part of modern life, even movies and emojis. But there is not enough proof to back it up. We are still victims of our own unscientific biases. But there's another consideration that needs inspection.

Not many studies have examined how people combine knowledge from different types of expression and how this combined understanding affects conclusions. Even though different modalities have similar (social) effects on observers, it is not clear which one or more modalities mainly determine how observers feel, especially when different modalities seem at odds with each other, like when someone hides an emotion in their voice but still shows it on their face.

AI has not been trained to consider the facial, vocal, and physical behavioral indicators potentially revealing a person's emotional state. Of course, to do this requires more than just facial recognition software, but that isn't a major issue since people can easily be scanned into a program.

AI is fast approaching an ability to detect emotion or, possibly, instances intended to deceive. As it is trained on more and more data and databases, its power in this area will increase exponentially. At this point, artificial intelligence is still in its toddlerhood, and adulthood is fast approaching us. But we still must contend with the biases that may have been entered into the training, without realization, by the trainers.

Chapter 10: The Medically Assisted Dying Issue Must Be Considered

L ife is a precious gift that those in healthcare feel committed to prolonging, even in the face of withering odds of patient suffering or being placed in a coma or other extraordinary measures to keep them alive. We are not taught to help people end their lives, and this has traditionally been seen by religions as a sin, by legal authorities as a crime, and by healthcare professionals as unethical. The worldview regarding assisted dying by medical professionals, however, has been changing over the past several decades, and some countries have initiated laws toward that end.

In 11 of the 50 U.S. states (as of 2023), adults may receive medical help to end their lives. Doctors in Washington, DC, can write prescriptions for drugs that people can self-administer because of the *Death With Dignity Act 2016*. Now, more laws have been passed that permit more types of healthcare workers in that district to approve requests for medically assisted death. The drugs can also be mailed to patients instead of having to be picked up in person.

.When physician-assisted death (PAD) has been facilitated, it has been when the patient had no hope of survival or was in such intense pain that medication could not ease it. Before that time, patients with no prospects of survival were placed in hospice care, where they were made comfortable with medications and could continue their lives as they wished. My mother was placed in one of the first hospice units in New York City. It was a blessing for our family and a relief for our beloved mother.

But hospice isn't the only thing that healthcare considers when death is inevitable. Now, there is even a change in terms of mental health.

As more and more countries allow it, physician-assisted death for people with a psychiatric illness remains a controversial issue. People must be able to make their own decisions about PAD, and their pain must be unbearable and cannot be relieved.

Patients with psychiatric disorders have been able to receive PAD in the Netherlands since the 1990s. This makes it one of the few countries that talk about the treatment from real-life experience.

We do have advance care directives that specifically lay out the terms under which no extraordinary steps are to be taken to extend a dying person's life. The NIA has a downloadable guide on the subject.

However, fearing lawsuits, hospitals and professionals have disregarded these directives and continued with heroic measures, often in the face of a family's wishes to abide by the directive.

I have seen this in action when a man was dying and in great pain. The staff hooked him up to all the machines that preserve life and refused to listen to his daughter, who said he had a directive. They went on working until he died. What had they done for the patient and his family? No one needs to tell any of us. Two other relatives were "made comfortable" by their in-hospital physicians.

Patients with psychiatric disorders have been able to get PAD in the Netherlands since the 1990s. This makes it one of the few countries to talk about the treatment from real-life experience. Many of the books that talk about these events can only be found in Dutch. It is against the law in the Netherlands to help someone kill someone else. However, doctors will not be charged if they follow the "Due Care Criteria" set out in the "Termination of Life on Request and Assisted Suicide Review Act."

Medicine is now emerging in many ways, and one of them is palliative psychiatry, where there is an admission by the provider and the patient that treatment of all kinds has not been effective. Certainly, psychiatry has seen any attempts at suicide or aiding in someone's death to be anathema to its mission of life-saving.

Some people with severe and long-lasting mental illness do not get to a point where they are happy with their mental health, psychosocial functioning, or quality of life, even with the best care. With each failed treatment try, the chance of reducing symptoms goes down while the chance of experiencing physical or mental side effects goes up. There have been calls for palliative methods of care to be used in psychiatry because the benefit-harm ratio of treatments meant to reduce symptoms is getting worse.

The American Medical Association, regarding their stance on palliative psychiatry, has issued: "All general medical, surgical, and psychiatric patients deserve palliative approaches to their care. Palliative psychiatry, especially, deserves clinical and ethical attention because of its promise as an emerging field renewing attention to patients whose illnesses—such as treatment-resistant depression—and symptoms—such as persistent suicidality—challenge our faith in health care as a life-affirming source of hope."

Not everyone agrees that palliative psychiatry is acceptable. People have supported the part of MAiD that says people with serious illnesses that cannot be cured have the moral right to avoid shame and pain. From a professional and moral perspective, some argue that the practice is unethical. Some people say that psychological MAiD is not ethical because it is not possible to tell if a mental illness can not be effectively treated. Research, after all, is making major strides in medications, but how long can someone wait?

We have read various media outlets' articles on people with psychiatric disorders having medical help in their deaths. The disorders have a wide range, from severe major depression, anorexia nervosa, personality disorders, and other disorders. Each article that appears may initially shock the reader. Still, we must be sensitive to the needs of the individual and ensure that all precautions are taken so that we thoroughly understand the intention of that individual and that they are not being coerced or in any way pushed.

Life is still seen as precious, and death is inevitable, but that end can be of our own choosing under specific circumstances. Certainly, we would not support the flippant request of someone who is bored (and a very famous actor committed suicide because he said life was boring). Still, besides physical pain, there can be intolerable mental pain.

I once saw a psychiatric patient in a hospital who begged me to end his suffering. I saw another psychiatric patient in a different hospital who had such severe physical and cognitive impairment (he had worked as a top government official abroad), and he *attempted suicide at least four times.* The last I heard, he tried three more times, and he had succeeded. For them, there was only a daily existence, which meant yet more mental pain.

Cultures are changing, and with them will come sweeping changes in how we live our lives and make our laws. For all of us, this is a time for mindfulness in an area where all of us are involved.

Chapter 11: Danger in Cosmetics Could Mean Cancer in the Future

G eology and cosmetics have come to a crash point because an ingredient in many of the expensive cosmetics women use daily contains a naturally occurring ingredient that can cause cancer: talc. A number of luxury brand cosmetics companies have or still use talc in their products.

As students of oceanography and geology, we were taught that the natural element in rock formations also contains a highly dangerous bit of material, talc, that can cause cancer. Talc may contain asbestos, naturally, which, when introduced into the lungs, is like tiny needles that penetrate and remain and cause cancer. How many women have used products over the years, especially on their babies and in their cosmetics, without knowing their potential danger?

When was the last time you scrutinized the ingredient list of products you use on your body or face? That long listing may contain talc and asbestos, which may be found in health supplements, so look carefully before you buy. However, the asbestos in the talc will not be a listed ingredient.

Even the most expensive top brands of any item may contain talc as an ingredient, so don't feel reassured when the label is well-known and expensive because they use talc, too. Some cosmetic manufacturers now tout their products as free from talc to address consumers' concerns.

Cosmetics and their chemicals, besides color additives, do not have to be reviewed or approved by the FDA before being sold. This is because of the Federal Food, Drug, and Cosmetic Act (FD&C Act). Cosmetics must have the right information on the label and be safe for people to use as directed on the label or as is usual. But is it sufficient that something is on the label, not reviewed by the FDA, and found to be a danger to health and still be sold to unaware consumers?

To protect consumers from harmful chemicals in cosmetics and personal care items, the Cosmetic, Toiletry, and Fragrances Association (CTFA) released voluntary guidelines in 1976. They said that all talc used in cosmetics in the US should not contain any asbestos that could be detected. The interesting item is how the talc is tested because methods vary, and not all asbestos may be found.

In a nationwide deal, Johnson & Johnson has agreed to pay $700 million to settle claims that it lied to customers in its advertising about the safety of its talcum-based powder products.

The health products giant will no longer produce, market, or sell any baby powder or other body or cosmetic products that contain talcum powder as part of the settlement, which the court has not yet approved.

Most of the worries about a link between talcum powder and cancer have been about people who breathe in talc particles at work, like talc miners, having a higher chance of getting lung cancer. But that's not the extent of asbestos exposure because consumer use also varies. The dangers of talc were first published in 1898 in a text on mineralogy.

If you regularly use talcum powder in your private area, it might raise your risk of getting ovarian cancer.

The Food and Drug Administration (FDA) and the talc industry say that talc has not contained asbestos since 1976, when the talc industry set a voluntary standard for the amount of asbestos in cosmetic powder. However, additional proof shows that cosmetic talc has always had asbestos.

Lawsuits against companies that use talc in their products have been filed against numerous companies, including:

Avon makes makeup based on talcum. More than 100 people were being sued by Avon because its talc products contained asbestos.

A California jury gave a 76-year-old woman with mesothelioma $53.3 million in 2022. That amount included $10.3 million in punitive damages.

The company that makes the talcum-based body powder Cashmere Bouquet is Colgate-Palmolive.

The following products have been mentioned in several talc cases:

$2.1 billion to 22 women who sued Johnson & Johnson for ovarian cancer in a baby powder lawsuit

• $72.5 million to rubber stamp workers who got lung cancer after being exposed to asbestos in products

• $30 million to the wife of an Illinois worker who got cancer from handling asbestos-contaminated talcum powder at a tire factory

• $20 million to the widow of a Rhode Island man who died in 2020 from mesothelioma years after working with asbestos-contaminated talc

You do not have to use cosmetic talc. There is a safe and useful alternative. In 1977, one company looked at the pros and cons of cornstarch and talc powders and discovered that women "overall rate cornstarch significantly higher." Corn starch is not known to cause any kind of cancer.

Physicians have been telling patients not to use cosmetic talc since the 1960s because it clearly causes harm, like asphyxiation and talcosis, and raises the risk of cancer. They back laws that make it illegal to use talc in cosmetic powders. Researchers must keep looking into and publishing cases of ongoing regulatory oversight and internal conversations. This will help people improve government agency oversight.

The concern with all cosmetic products must continue, and consumers must ensure that they receive accurate information whenever they purchase any cosmetic or hygienic product. The dangers not listed in the ingredients are not apparent, and consumers are left to protect themselves by education.

Chapter 12: Hazing Has a Disturbing History and Must Be Stopped

Traditions may be fine and may forge the bonds needed for groups to remain vital and cohesive, but one of the traditions, hazing, remains a serious concern. The media has carried articles about the sudden deaths of pledges to fraternities, and, as a result, universities have outlawed much of this activity. What's more, legal action and lawsuits may be brought against the groups or individuals involved. But there are places where it is still acceptable behavior—one is law enforcement, and another is military service.

There was a great deal of attention paid to the stunts shown on various video platforms when kids were attempting to perform stunts or eat incredibly spicy hot peppers. The stunts may have played a role in some aspects of hazing. YouTube has now banned dangerous stunts, but hazing with deadly effects still persists. No, hazing doesn't appear in these videos, but who knows if groups don't video their victims for future "enjoyment."

I was once in a group therapy class during my doctoral studies where a young woman had recently joined the police force. Her fellow officers decided she needed to know her place. One day, into her first week, she opened her locker and found it contained a large quantity of feces. After that, she experienced other incidents that she didn't wish to disclose.

But hazing isn't only in the US because the media has reported it worldwide. One instance in Russia stands out for special note. The military member's defense team at his trial "*has said their client went on a shooting spree in October 2019, killing eight fellow soldiers—including two high-ranking officers—in the town of Gorny in the Zabaikalye region after he was tortured and beaten by other soldiers and officers during his induction into the service.*"

The Marines have traditionally "pinned" a member by forcing a pin through the recruit's clothing and into his skin. This practice has since been discontinued. But Parris Island had other stories for reporters, as well, when it came to a specific Muslim recruit. He died after a mysterious fall at the facility and may have been a victim of brutal hazing.

A recent hazing incident was reported to me, and it may serve as a current illustration of how hazing has squirreled itself into the ranks of upper military who supervise high school ROTC members. Remember, the military is ripe for marketing to increase recruitment, and high schools are prime recruiting territory. Who wouldn't want to be in a spot where you can join the military of your choice, say the Air Force, do your stint, and come out to make over $200K a year flying planes for corporations?

Hazing seems to be a part of it, but "recruits" never expect that and gleefully accept everything their recruiter tells them, one of which is the huge salary they'll make after their service. Is it true? Ask former military personnel.

Bullying recruits and high school students, too, can lead to mental health issues, not stronger military members. In fact, brutality and hazing appear to be part of military strategy in some areas. Sexual harassment is also part of the equation.

A quite young ROTC member made the unpardonable mistake of placing his elbows on the table as he ate. Shocked and loaded for bear, the older members decided it was time for action, humiliation, and bullying. He had to be forced to drink a concoction of seltzer and extra hot sauce until he threw up all over his uniform.

The young man brought the situation to his grandparent/guardian, who contacted the colonel in charge, who told her that it was what they do. He didn't say they'd stop it or take any action; it was part of being in ROTC. Technically, I would suppose this is a misdemeanor assault if a charge were filed with the local police.

I have to wonder how the colonel's superior views his actions. And how far do they go in this hazing? Is it restricted to making a "recruit" drink a hot pepper drink to the point of vomiting all over, or does it get worse from there?

Perhaps the military needs to review who is in charge of local high school ROTC units and get them to go over the guidelines regarding the treatment of members and how hazing is forbidden. And make sure that the colonel has some re-education classes as well.

Chapter Thirteen

Chapter 13: AI Can Outwrite Shakespeare and Remain Hidden?

AI writing is no longer in the elementary-school era, and LLMs are steadily advancing their ability to become more humanlike than previously. Even new AI detection tools may not be able to identify AI from human efforts, as new research indicates.

As of 2024, the sophistication of AI-generated books and articles is rising rapidly. Of major concern is that AI-generated research poses ethical concerns in academia, where originality is paramount, making it challenging to produce truly undetectable work. But it is also a concern for anyone who is a professional writer or aspires to be one, as well as MFA programs in colleges.

In two separate studies, participants who were not trained poetry readers failed to recognize AI-generated poems at a rate higher than chance (46.6%, N= 16,340). Notably, when asked to identify the author of a poem, participants were more likely to respond that a person rather than an AI wrote it.

AI-generated poems were mistaken for human-written poetry because they scored higher on rhythm and elegance. Due to the similarity between human and AI poetry, participants may have confused the simplicity of AI poetry with human complexity.

Why Poetry May Be Safe From AI

On the other hand, AI-written poetry might not be a threat to poetry writing in most cases. Some have stated that no matter how good LLMs are at writing different types of content, they will never be able to produce poetry of any quality because poetry is all about meaning and creativity, and AI-generated prose is boring and lacks imagination. Poetry's subjective nature, defying strict criteria and often inverting meaning, makes it difficult to understand and analyze, especially for non-experts. AI follows rules and its learning and neither fit into human poetry writing; creativity is key here.

What did one study propose? Is it that poems created by AI were more popular? It could be that the simplicity of AI poetry is a contributing factor to its higher overall rating across all measures. The study found that AI-generated poems were easier to understand and relate to than human-authored poetry. When asked to explain their reactions, participants used the phrase "makes little sense" more frequently when explaining poems written by humans. Metaphors and complexity, again, are easier to process than human text and may make reading poetry simpler for readers who wish for simplicity.

So, while poetry may seem to be a challenge for AI, the fact that it beat Shakespeare in writing poetry should give us pause. Anyone can use LLMs to imitate any writer, including us, which means they could pass off work written by an LLM as their own. If we wanted Hemingwayesque writing, we could do it. Is this writing as we would like it to remain, or is it the inauthenticity that we find in painters who copy great works of art? We've seen them sitting, sometimes, in museums where they are copying a painting.

Where Are LLMs Going Regarding Writing?

Researchers investigating LLMs and their creative writing capabilities beyond poetry in 2024 are primarily focused on determining the limits of these programs. They are parsing out crafting intricate plots, developing compelling characters, and capturing nuanced human emotions in fiction, including short stories and longer works.

Evidence suggests that LLMs frequently produce formulaic and predictable narratives, devoid of the unique ideas and varied viewpoints present in works of creative writing by humans. Their training data is to blame for this, since it encourages the use of clichés and tropes. But in the world of AI, nothing is stagnant and learning marches on.

A significant challenge for LLMs is the construction of complex plotlines with interesting conflicts and unexpected turns, which frequently leads to predictable and linear narrative structures. Computer engineers are looking at ways to improve the collaborative creative process by guiding LLMs to generate more imaginative and interesting stories through prompts and user feedback.

In addition, research is looking into new ways to train LLMs on more complicated and varied literary data, such as world-building, character-arc analysis, and theme exploration components. All the elements are there, and the training to produce them is being created.

Prompts are the wave of the future, and programs exist to help writers develop better prompts for their original work through algorithms. A quick look at YouTube videos will reveal how to get hundreds of prompts from someone or how to write better prompts. Currently, programs can provide precise titles for creative work, outlines for articles or stories, and immediate rewrites for something provided seconds ago. The programs never tire, but the tokens do pile up.

What is a token? They are the equivalent of bits of text that writers pay for (in paid programs), which can be thousands of words per month. Yes, tokens are the wave of the here-and-now and the future. If you use up your tokens, you can buy more to keep writing with the AI programs, most of which may keep your content on the cloud rather than on your computer.

For anyone strapped for funds, some free programs will provide you with monthly tokens (often around 3K). Free programs can summarize or write content based on research articles you upload. This can be invaluable to anyone who needs research summaries quickly and can be an important educational assist to students. As Sal Khan (developer of The Khan Academy) believes, AI may save education.

Writing will not be solely the province of AI or computer engineers, but they can provide new tools to make writing more provocative, informative, and smoother. Effort in individual input in our writing remains a given, even when AI is providing content for us. Everyone knows about programs that catch AI-produced products, but that old adage, don't throw the baby out with the dishwater, still applies. Use AI intelligently, and it can make all of us better writers.

Chapter 14: Angry and Upset? How About Your Emotional Lifesaver, Mindfulness?

Since Jon Kabot-Zinn and his fellow researchers first suggested mindfulness, an adaptation of centuries-old techniques in Asia, to the Western world, it has been a topic of active exploration in countless articles, books, seminars, and therapy sessions. It has been a staple of New Age psychology and a form of self-help to deal with stressful situations or emotional subjects.

There is a wealth of knowledge available on the subject, and thousands of research papers and research projects have delved into the utility of this technique in both mental and physical areas of exploration. However, not everyone is convinced that it is as effective as we believe, and there seems to be some disagreement.

Although authors may disagree, we must examine the current research, especially that into physical medicine, where mindfulness is extremely helpful to patients. Specifically, hypertension remains a serious medical disorder that requires more than medication for its control.

In the United States, high blood pressure has cost $53.2 billion a year over the last few decades. Getting control of high blood pressure would have a significant effect on death from cardiovascular disease (CVD) than eliminating any other CVD risk factor in women and any risk factor in men except smoking.

Blood pressure that is too high must be addressed to improve people's health. We know a great deal about what causes it. For example, food, exercise, alcohol use, and taking antihypertensive drugs as prescribed are all big factors that affect blood pressure. But figures from around the world show that only about half of the people with high blood pressure have it under control. Hypertension is now one of the most important noncommunicable diseases to treat and avoid around the world.

People over 65 who had isolated systolic hypertension that was challenging to treat received relaxed response training. The people in the study were more likely to be able to control their blood pressure, and some of them might have been able to cut back on or even stop taking their blood pressure medicines. What happens during this exercise?

While the body relaxes, blood pressure drops, inflammation and blood vessel tightness slow down, and blood vessels widen. This effect seems to be caused by nitric oxide, a molecule that our bodies make that helps keep blood pressure in check by relaxing and widening blood vessels. The results would seem to be quite dramatic.

But it's not only cardiac issues that may be addressed by mindfulness training because it has been used in stress as well. A large project looked at how well single, short mindfulness interventions worked in a multi-site study that took place at 37 sites and had 2,239 valid observations. The researchers discovered that mindfulness exercises—body scan, mindful breathing, mindful walking, and loving-kindness—helped people feel less stressed than a control group.

Exercise and Eating, Too

One study found that combining physical activity (PA) with mindfulness-based intervention (MBI) provided a positive feedback loop. When used together in interventions, PA and MBIs may have bigger benefits than either one alone, probably because of working together in ways that complement each other. For example, mindfulness training might make it easier to start doing PA by teaching people to accept and not judge their possibly uncomfortable experiences. On the other hand, doing PA can increase a person's sense of accomplishment and motivation to keep doing it.

Can mindfulness help with other issues? It seems to be able to be used in aiding people with their eating habits. The MB-BP (Mindfulness-Blood Pressure) program might help people change the way they eat, which is one of the main causes of high blood pressure.

Even though the Dietary Approaches to Stop Hypertension (DASH) plan can lower blood pressure (BP), most people do not follow it very well. Mindfulness training that is tailored to promoting healthy habits that lower blood pressure may help people stick to the DASH diet, in part by raising their interoceptive awareness of what they are eating.

DIY Mindfulness

Anyone who is unfamiliar with mindfulness may find these three Mayo Clinic outlines helpful:

Meditation with a body scan: Put your arms at your sides and your legs out in front of you. Your hands should face up. Pay careful attention to each part of your body one at a time, going from toe to head or head to toe. Be aware of any feelings, thoughts, or sensations that each part of your body brings up.

Meditation while sitting: Hold your hands in your lap and keep your back straight. Your feet should be flat on the floor. Pay attention to how your breath moves in and out of your body as you breathe through your nose. If thoughts or feelings come up during your meditation, write them down, and then focus on your breath again.

Meditation while walking: Start walking slowly in a quiet area 10 to 20 feet long. Pay attention to how walking and standing feel and to the small moves that help you stay balanced. When you get to the end, turn around and keep walking while paying attention to how you feel. In fact, new research has attested to slow walking as opposed to jogging, so there's an additional plus here. And it may even help with weight loss.

Is mindfulness something anyone can do whenever they want? It would seem so and the benefits are great, plus there's no need to enroll in special programs or limit it to a specific time frame—it's at your disposal every day of the week for how long you want to maintain its use. But using it regularly appears to be a good thing, so it might be something to consider.

Chapter 15: Money May Be the Root of All Evil, But It Can Bring Happiness

How many of us have heard the expression, "Money is the root of all evil?" It denigrates money, but it also does something else; it denies a person's ability to discern good from evil. Without offering a path for charitable pursuits and philanthropic endeavors, it portrays money as a dangerous course leading to moral decline.

We have to wonder what the likes of Andrew Carnegie, and the titans of business who have had museums, universities, and medical schools named after them, thought of their vast wealth. Were the donations a means of gaining income tax advantages or creating a place in perpetuity for themselves? Or did they have a need and a wish to perpetuate culture and learning, and was their money the means to do this?

Thinking of money and lots of it, brings thoughts of both charity and selfishness, and, in my mind, the Charles Dickens story, "*A Christmas Carol.*" Dickens not only brings us into the home of a humble accountant, working for a selfish, nasty, very wealthy old man, but has sparked something new in research called "*The Scrooge Factor.*" When does Scrooge decide to become a more giving, lovable individual? It comes once he is reminded of his mortality and how being alone at this special time of the year is terrifying for him. Has Scrooge's money made him happy? That's doubtful.

Terror management theory says that people deal with the anxiety that can come from knowing that death is inevitable by hanging on to sources of value that are important to them in their culture. One source of value is helping others; studies have shown that being reminded of death makes people want to help others more. Sounds like Scrooge, doesn't it? But there's something else at work here, too.

When someone is materialistic, they value their belongings highly. While people who believe in high materialism keep looking for happiness in things like money, status, and looks, people who believe in self-determination theory (SDT) say that they should meet their basic psychological needs for autonomy, competence, and relatedness in order to be happy. Although materialism is an example of an external drive, it can make it hard to meet psychological needs, which can then hurt one's own well-being.

Now, the emphasis is more on subjective well-being and what makes us happy or motivates us. As well as overall evaluations, measures of well-being capture judgments of life happiness or fulfillment.

These judgments can be applied to specific parts of life, like relationships, community, health, or work.

Happiness, therefore, isn't constrained by money but by our overall feeling of happiness, which is a conglomeration of many aspects of our lives, money being only one of them and how money contributes to all the others. Are we happier with money? Undoubtedly, it plays a major role in many aspects of our lives, and we can't deny that, but making it the primary reason to exist in our lives would seem shortsighted.

There are, however, studies that show money can contribute to happiness. It is often found that as income goes up, so does a person's level of well-being. Do people who make more money feel better? There is a pattern where the average happiness number goes up until a certain income level and then stays the same. But some research indicates it continues to improve with more money. The question remains regarding where individual changes take place in money's role in the lives of the wealthy and how they use money.

Researchers have found that there are two types of well-being (happiness): experienced well-being and reflective well-being. Experienced well-being is how people feel during the moments of their lives. People who make more money feel better every day and are happier with their lives. Being assured of our ability to pay the expenses of our lives and contribute to that of others would certainly give us a sense of satisfaction, aka happiness.

Reflecting on ourselves helps us better understand ourselves, which in turn helps us value our unique point of view more. So, thinking about who we are and what is important to us and enjoying our successes can help us determine how to protect and improve our health and happiness. It's not always money, but what we can do with it and how it may help us design a path in our lives toward achieving happiness and avoiding that "evil" one.

There is no doubt about it: money helps. No one would deny its role in our lives or the fact that without it, motivation can increase or be crushed.

Chapter 16: Psychotherapy Shouldn't Be Fatal, But Lethal Fraud Still Exists

Thousands of people worldwide are in need of mental health services, but in many areas, adequately trained and appropriately certified professionals are not available. When this happens, this may be fertile ground for fraudsters who promise to cure any mental health or physical illness with unique, fraudulent "therapies" that do nothing but scam the patients who come to them. There are even those in the field who have licenses in mental healthcare and who hang out shingles that present them in a manner that is not appropriate to their licensing.

I recall one man who put a sign on his lawn and in his office that he was "Dr." when, in fact, he had a master's degree. This fraud was included on his letterhead, where he put a number that appeared to any unaware person to be a licensed number. It was not his license at all but a number for some other activity in which he engaged.

The licensing board had repeatedly warned him to rectify the situation, but he didn't because he knew that there wasn't enough staff to go out and check on his actions. Everyone thought he was a medical doctor or a psychiatrist in the town where he practiced.

Another large practice had secretaries administering psychological test materials for which they neither had experience nor degrees. Ethically, they should not have had access to these materials.

Everyone who came to the practice was put through a series of computerized tests, and their insurance was charged for all of this unnecessary testing. The practice reaped millions of dollars a year, and nothing was ever done to the man who owned it. He even charged insurance for missed therapy sessions, which is outright insurance fraud.

The secretary administered a basic IQ test at another office, not a therapy office, but offering a different service. The testing material was kept on her desk. Nothing was ever done about this, either because the man in charge was not a licensed healthcare professional, and he was never investigated for this practice.

Anyone wishing to check on a licensed mental health counselor can go to the state-by-state listing on the Internet. For licensed psychologists, there is also a similar listing. Psychiatrists are listed as medical doctors.

Then, there are those who call themselves doctors who may have degrees in things other than healthcare-related specialties, such as administration or even history. The term is not carefully regulated and may be used by so many people that it is, and can, intend to deceive.

There are also those who catfish on the Internet and present themselves as something other than who they truly are. I am speaking about authors who delve into the intimate, personal lives of young people and then use this material to write books. Is it ethical? Do these people really respond to anything regarding ethics? I find it absolutely untenable.

What about those who "graduated" from schools that have been shut down because they were nothing but diploma mills? Yes, they are out there, and when they write their website profiles, they carefully exclude any mention of the school and say they have "studied" topics such as neurobiology or science.

Taking one course could be seen as "studying." Are they experts in any area? Deceit and deception are their watchwords, and you are their intended victims. Bestseller means nothing. Please do not be misled by this term.

Defrauding Patients and Insurance

I've written about this before, but the material requires updating because these practices continue to emerge and must be dealt with legally.

Today, we are still confronted by those who would deceive us and, by doing so, become extremely wealthy, but the consequences for the people who come to them can be fatal. These individuals sought help after they believed there was no help from traditional sources of medicine or therapy, and they came wanting to believe that these "healers" offered the only hope for these patients.

Now, the curtain is being pulled back, and lawsuits and legal battles are being fought as some people have died. One man has now been charged with more than one incident of manslaughter when he advised someone to stop taking their insulin and instead use his "slapping" therapy. The man died.

Federal charges say a woman from Minnesota sold a fake "microcurrent therapy" device across the country that she said could fix almost any illness or condition but actually burned or hurt people who tried to use it

Not only are these fake healers being uncovered, but those who promote unprofessional therapies that no professional organizations recognize are being outed, too. Unfortunately, once their papers were published, too many people readily picked them up and used them as references in their papers.

Can you imagine that up to 10,000 professionally published papers had to be retracted for various forms of data manipulation or outright fraud? This form of publication pollution takes time to discover, but once it is discovered, we know that the damage has been done to too many people.

One form of alleged therapy is conversion therapy, which claims to change people's sexual orientation from homosexual to heterosexual. Every professional organization has debunked this, and it is no longer viewed as valid by anyone but the practitioners who make money from it. How many people have been psychologically damaged by this therapy that perpetuates feelings of shame?

There are no magic healers out there, but they will continue presenting themselves as such, and it is up to consumers to check everyone's background carefully. Criminals are always looking for new ways to make money and unfortunate, hopeless

Chapter 17: Look for the Positive Side of Boredom and Benefit From It

B oredom can be a friend or a foe, and we are the ones who will determine how we view it and how we may benefit ourselves and our children from it. It is not a state of inertia where we are devoid of everything and every creative aspect of our lives, but one that offers opportunity if we perceive it when it presents itself.

How often have we heard a small child look at us and say, "I'm bored! " And how did we respond to that? Behind that one word is a nexus of learning and a kernel of inspiration.

We all get bored sometimes, and it makes us feel uncomfortable. We may believe that we should do something, that we're missing something, or that there may be some lack in ourselves. These are several perspectives on the situation we find ourselves in, but we should not despair because research is pointing the way, and we can follow it to a happier, more productive, and more creative life.

As the right to pursue one's happiness and sense of "self" became a universally recognized human value, ennui became prominent in Western philosophical thought. Many people believe it is a negative emotion that prevents happiness when we have to sit through a tedious meeting, do the same thing repeatedly, or be in an uninteresting environment.

Boredom has a bad rap because it is strongly correlated with undesirable actions. But it is also a really essential feeling when we cannot get ourselves engrossed in something or keep ourselves busy, no matter how much we try. On top of that, it is associated with daydreaming and mental idleness, both of which can spark creativity and new ideas or motivate us to do important things. If we see boredom as a beginning rather than a stagnant time, it is a world-opening opportunity.

When Do We Get Bored and Who Gets Bored?

Researchers have examined what happens when we feel bored. On the one hand, we experience boredom when we are not challenged enough; on the other hand, we experience boredom when something is excessively demanding, like a rigorous university lecture. Boredom may result if the material is over our heads.

But there's also another explanation for degrees of boredom. According to the Goldilocks Principle, which specifies an ideal level of involvement, a state of boredom indicates that we are not engaging to our full potential. Some people experience boredom more frequently than others, which is also explained by applying a framework.

We all set our own framework for what is just right versus what is not good enough. It goes back to the old children's story about the three bears and their beds and how there was one that had just the right softness. According to this reasoning, each of us sets the standard for boredom, and it's not the situation necessarily, but a bit of perfectionism on our part.

But there isn't one type of boredom, but two. One is state boredom, the temporary experience of being bored in certain situations, such as having nothing to do in an uninspiring situation or performing the same simple task repeatedly. The other aspect is boredom as an innate trait, the individual's proneness to boredom. High boredom proneness has been associated with ADHD, risk-taking behaviors, a higher risk of dropping out of school, and mental symptoms such as apathy, depression, anxiety, and substance abuse.

1. **Turning Boredom Into a Positive**: After a period of intense activities, the brain needs a bit of rest and a time to kick back. During this time, we may experience a sensation of boredom, so use it, and instead of being bored, take it under your control. Here are a few simple things that you can do:

2. **Balance what you do with time to rest**: It is helpful to have a range of things that you enjoy, that let you interact with other people, and that keep your mind active. Still, taking breaks is important for keeping your brain fresh. Try to balance planned tasks and short breaks to improve your creative thinking.

3. **Do something different:** To stay creative and avoid boredom, join a club, try a new sport, play a game, read a book, or cook a new recipe. Of course, this all depends on when you are feeling bored and have the freedom to enter into something new. Obviously, boredom

at a corporate meeting or in a lecture hall differs from boredom that you may experience at home.

4. Go outside: Being outside is one of the best ways to relax and avoid boredom. It also helps you work on new ideas. We know that being outdoors and even walking in a park can boost your mood and your creativity and turn a boring time into one of promise.

5. **Accept that you are curious** and kind, and allow your mind to daydream: In fact, daydreaming has been found to be extremely valuable in coming up with creative solutions to problems and in any type of new creative activity. Allow your mind to wander.

6. **Enjoy remembering things:** Older people spend a lot of time thinking about the past. There is nothing wrong with this. If thinking about the past too much becomes a problem, try focusing for a few minutes on your present or future goals and dreams. Think about the possibilities in life that are yet to come, and perhaps begin putting a plan into action.

What About Kids and Boredom?

Boredom can be a time of unseen brain development as children begin to engage in new, simple but creative tasks. Setting aside time for kids to be bored requires planning and practice. Researchers suggest a few ways to add some order to kids' free time instead of telling them to keep busy for two hours or letting them use screens while they are not doing anything.

If kids do not know what to do first, adults can suggest a few things to do, like building a fort indoors or outside, an obstacle course, or a fairy garden. But the point is to be as broad as possible.

The people who care for children, especially their parents, are likely to have the most impact on their behavior, both genetically (innately) and environmentally. Studies have indicated that a person's tendency to become bored may not be solely genetic, and how they handle boredom may depend on their upbringing.

They can strengthen their skills, imagination, and self-esteem by being bored. Talk to them about the things they love and are interested in. Then, you can list short-term and long-term projects together so they have something to do when they are bored.

Mostly, little kids need a variety of short tasks to pick from. Things like art projects, dressing up, and playing sports outside can be on their list. Kids who are older can work on bigger projects, like planting a garden, or be given a bunch of DIY leftovers and told to "make" something new. This is a challenge that kids can love.

I remember a friend's father, who made it a practice to always help kids build small things and then encourage them to improve on anything that they had created, such as a small, simple float for a pond. He even built a backyard tightrope with a thick cable he had found somewhere. It was only a foot off the ground, so kids could learn to walk on it safely.

Every child who entered his backyard was captivated by his creativity, leaving with new ideas and a renewed joy of learning. I remember him taking a group of us to teach us how to skin dive. Then he began building surfboards, and he taught some kids in a group how to surf. There was never a dull moment with him.

Nobody should perceive boredom as a waste of time unless they actively choose to do so. It can be a time for wonder.

Chapter 18: Psychiatry, the Law, and MSP Spell Murder

The law is quite clear: murder is a crime, and criminals must be punished, except when they're not, and therein lies a dichotomy that has been forged by a person's ability to hire high-powered lawyers. Not all victims deserve additional punishment at the hands of the law, but that thorny statement will be the source of heated debates as we go on.

No, murder may not be what is considered a suitable topic for any time, but when it is a New Year, we want resolutions, fancifully looking backward at our actions, and hope for the future. But there are questions that cry out for consideration no matter the time of year, and this is one of them. The case in point is Gypsy Rose Blanchard.

Blanchard, whose mother pulled her out of school in the second grade, indicating that her daughter had serious medical illnesses that required her to remain at home, is the case in point. Her mother, Dee Dee, made Gypsy Blanchard take unnecessary medication and endure unnecessary medical procedures; the medication was the reason why Gypsy Blanchard's teeth fell out. The windows of the home were blacked out to avoid detection. No social work outreach for a sickly child that can't attend school? Should the school nurse have been involved?

In fact, the mother forced the young girl to use a wheelchair and feeding tube to reinforce the false claims that the girl not only had muscular dystrophy but a variety of other illnesses. Whenever medical professionals grew suspicious, the mother used the usual action of those with **Munchausen's Syndrome by Proxy** relied on—switching healthcare providers or even towns for medical services.

From the sheriff's office, which looked into health concerns regarding Gypsy Blanchard five years earlier, to groups like *Habitat for Humanity,* which provided the Blanchards with their Volunteer Way home, the woman reportedly conned everyone.

I recall one of the first professional articles I wrote was on MSP, and I only wrote it after attending a seminar where it was mentioned—the first time I had ever heard about it. Afterward, I would become more sensitized to the issue and the pathology involved in it.

In my opinion, the mother's actions of constantly changing providers alone mandate a national database for suspicious medical cases. Isn't this how we now catch serial murderers?

Succinctly stated, as the girl grew older and realized her hopeless situation as a medical prisoner in her home, she enlisted the aid of an internet boyfriend who killed her mother. The girl was, ultimately, arrested, pled guilty, and sent to prison. Her boyfriend is serving a life sentence for the murder.

What about the young victim of a pedophile in prison in Massachusetts who killed his abuser? Should he be deported for his crime? He's not alone in being imprisoned for killing his abuser or the person who sexually trafficked them. Aren't they victims, or do we still stand by a rigid rule of punishment for these crimes despite extenuating circumstances?

Now, Blanchard has been released from prison and is about to be victimized yet again because her parole officer for the State of Missouri has decided she has to leave the state because she poses a danger. The reason? Her popularity. A three-part documentary about her story, The Prison Confessions of Gypsy Rose Blanchard, appeared on TV.

The case is a graphic illustration of how those with psychopathic intent can game the system. It should serve as a case to keep in mind whenever a patient with unpredictable, constantly changing, or incredibly unusual symptoms comes forward. But that is to say, extreme care must also be exercised to protect the innocent, who may be seen as concocting these illnesses, not limited to children but adults as well. Husbands have been found to perpetrate this on their wives, so mothers with kids or children with elderly parents are not the only ones guilty of these crimes.

Chapter 19: The One Medicine We Can All Freely Dispense — Hope

When someone gives up hope in the face of a medical illness, we are losing the battle—one that can be strengthened by maintaining a sense of hope even in the worst of times. Studies in science are starting to recognize the importance of hope and its promise in medicine.

In young adults with chronic illnesses, higher levels of hope are linked to better coping, well-being, and engagement in healthy behaviors. It also guards against depression and suicide. In teenagers, hope is associated with health, a sense of purpose, quality of life, and self-esteem. It is also essential for the development of resilience and maturity.

When we are faced with a chronic or life-threatening illness, hope can be an especially effective shield against the fear of the unknown. And it is the unknown that can be most upsetting when medical illness strikes.

Hope doesn't need to be focused on a cure, though those goals are appealing; instead, a person's hope can be directed toward finding comfort or joy. It can be nurtured and directed toward reaching life milestones, like meeting grandchildren or going to a child's wedding. Found in peaceful moments, too, hope is one thing we control.

Research indicates that hope is positively correlated with life satisfaction and acts as a buffer against the impact of negative and stressful life events. People high in hope tend to show better athletic, academic, occupational, and health outcomes. Hopeful people have positive thinking that is reflective of a realistic sense of optimism as well as the belief that they can produce routes to desired goals. These people see obstacles as challenges to overcome and are able to utilize their optimism to plan alternatives to achieve their end goal. Such a mindset serves us well in all aspects of our lives.

Hopelessness is primarily focused on goal blockage and motivational striving. Theorists of the Hopelessness Theory defined the construct of hopelessness as the negative expectation of highly desired outcomes along with the belief that one is helpless to bring about change in this situation. Hopelessness arises when a person's estimate of the probability of achieving specific goals is pessimistic, and they think that the plans of action in the pursuit of the goals are unlikely to lead to their attainment.

Even within certain patients with such serious illnesses as cancer, hope is proven to be a driver of life. Empirical research on cancer revealed that optimism was associated with a one-year survival rate in patients with head and neck cancer, as well as a greater capacity to handle stress; conversely, less optimistic cancer patients experienced more detrimental psychological changes.

Pessimistic attitudes were linked to worse physical health, an increased risk of depression, and higher death rates. Individuals with the inner drive to accomplish their goals and hope for the best outcomes might potentially live longer, healthier lives.

Additional research shows that optimism improves physical health outcomes for people with multiple sclerosis because it causes them to look for ways to improve their disease experiences and thrive in the face of adversity. It also reduces perfectionism, emotional anxiety, and non-adaptative attitudes toward chronic diseases in patients with ulcerative colitis and Crohn's disease.

While many studies have focused on younger populations, the results of research also indicate findings may have population-level implications, indicating the need for additional research. Although some public health practitioners may view "hope" as a concept outside of their purview, studies are highlighting associations between hope and a variety of outcomes related to social, mental, and physical well-being, suggesting that hope is an important area of future research and practice in public health.

Where do individuals begin? The area of most interest and help is positive thinking. Positive thinking is a mindset that approaches unpleasant situations in life in a more constructive and positive way, believing that the best will ultimately prevail rather than the worst.

Positive thinking frequently begins with self-talk, which is the ceaseless stream of unspoken, automatic thoughts that go through your mind. Some of these thoughts are based on logic and reason, while others are the result of misconceptions you create due to incomplete information or expectations based on preconceived notions about what might happen. The results of these studies have significant implications for older adult populations, as they broadly align with numerous studies that have focused on younger populations.

While medical research and psychotherapy are important spokes in the wheel of life, maintaining a sense of hope provides the framework of resilience and help for everyone.

Chapter 20: Women Are Pushed to "Idealized" Female Figures in Diet Wars

The diet industry and the media promoting its many products, programs, and entertainment stars involved in it are lucrative for corporations but can be injurious to women's mental and physical health. We now not only have plans that provide complete meals but also individual products aimed at keeping the culture of thinness in women alive, and an active customer base is vital.

How many fail at these programs is not discussed, only how happy a woman will be if she adheres to their mandates. Of course, cost is not the issue; meeting our cultural standards for a woman's body image is the main focus. And there are unseen dangers dieters may not see in their pursuit of the ideal body.

The risk of unhealthy diets and disordered eating patterns is higher in individuals with a negative body image. The effects of habitual social media use or exposure to image-related content on healthy young people's (18–30 years old) body image and food choices are still involved today, as we go from diets to pharmaceuticals.

The latest celebrity to admit that years of rigorous diet and exercise routines have not worked for her? Oprah Winfrey not only owns a major share of WeightWatchers but has now admitted she's on weight-control drugs but refuses to say which one. As she admitted, her days of fat-shaming are over. How will her revelation affect the sales of these drugs? It's another example of media exposure for a medication; this one was initially meant for those with diabetes.

But there may be health concerns related to these drugs, and we don't know about them for obvious reasons. Studies are lacking and may not be forthcoming. As a researcher noted in a media article, "You also have situations where you don't want to find adverse events if you're the manufacturer because you want to keep selling," and it's a liability. "So they're not saying they won't do it or couldn't be forced by the FDA to do it, but they're not rushing to do it on their own," he said. To date, these drugs sell more than the value of one European country's economy, and that should concern all of us.

I saw one woman in a weight-loss program lose 125 lbs., and she still wanted to lose more. When she was denied the shakes anymore, she said she'd buy them on the black market. There's a black market for diet shakes? The woman was slipping into anorexia.

Thirty studies of just over eleven thousand individuals indicated that participation in social media or exposure to image-related content was linked to increased levels of body dissatisfaction, overeating, dieting, and healthy food selection.

Diet culture has changed over the years, but its fundamental ideas—that is, a belief system that worships thinness and equates it with health and moral virtue—have remained the same. To be overweight is seen in a negative light, and only the diet matters because that's where salvation lies. There is never any consideration that the weight gain may not be under the woman's control or that factors other than diet may be in play; it's only what you eat. One word that you will see repeated is "control," and, of course, the result is "happiness," which will be achieved if you follow the diet. Failure is your fault.

Though they might not say it out loud, celebrities emphasize eating low in calories. They normalize fasting and restriction. They concentrate on things like detoxing. What does detoxing mean? To them, there is a mystery here that we have to solve (see "control" again).

Do they believe our bodies are storing "toxins," or is that their way of getting you to buy a product or try one of their unrealistic and unscientific approaches to health? Can it be dangerous to your health to follow these self-styled gurus of wellness? I think the true experts can tackle that one. Because someone is famous for something doesn't mean they're health experts; leave that to the dieticians. And 900 calories a day is a starvation diet and not healthy, no matter what celebrities tell you otherwise. And remember that celebrities undergo liposuction and gastric bypass without ever telling their fans.

Yes, most healthcare professionals know all about the starvation experiments run by Ancel Keys, Ph.D., known as the Minnesota Starvation Experiment, which provided advice on recuperation while illuminating the physical and mental damage brought on by malnutrition.

Maintaining a low weight is a way to elevate social status and demonize certain foods and eating styles while elevating others. Words like clean or healthy eating and wellness may be interspersed in the messages, but that's not the true target—purchasing a product remains paramount.

Another problematic means of dieting has also been identified. Weight cycling, which is another name for yo-yo eating or yo-yo dieting, is when you lose and gain weight over and over again. Each time you begin another of these cycles, it can become yet more difficult to lose weight the next time. It is, therefore, a losing proposition, and trying a new diet may not help, so don't believe the TV or media ads. This behavior has been linked to several psychological and physical problems.

People who engage in persistent diets and weight gain may experience feelings of worthlessness, failure, and unhappiness. Another common result of yo-yo dieting is the emergence of binge eating disorder.

The highly talented musician Karen Carpenter died as a result of anorexia when, again after a stint in rehab, she began to use a product known to cause weight loss but also cardiac arrest. During extreme caloric restriction, the body attempts to maintain itself by breaking down available protein in muscles, and the one muscle it attacks is the heart.

Yo-yo dieting has the potential to adversely affect the body's metabolism from a physiological perspective. Studies by the National Institute of Diabetes and Digestive and Kidney Diseases (NIDDK) and the American Heart Association (AHA) have shown that during the weight-regain phase, the body may become more adept at storing fat, which could make it more difficult to lose weight in the future.

This approach to dieting has also been connected to elevated cardiovascular disease risk factors. Variations in weight can affect insulin sensitivity, blood pressure, and cholesterol levels. The American Heart Association has stressed how crucial it is to keep a steady weight for cardiovascular health.

The cyclical nature of yo-yo dieting can negatively impact mental health from a psychological standpoint. People can feel remorseful and frustrated and have a poor opinion of themselves as failures. Studies that explore the psychological effects of weight cycling on mental health are published in journals such as the Journal of Consulting and Clinical Psychology.

Now, new research is looking backward at another approach to both dieting and the type of foods people who are overweight eat. The presence or absence of the neurotransmitter dopamine may be an issue, and that may lead to new treatments for the morbidly obese, but not for those who may engage in "unconscious" stress-related eating or eating lifestyles that result in overweight.

Whether it's biological, genetic, or a choice that results in weight control, the main lesson to be learned is that a "healthy" weight may be more your body's decision. Can you say it's out of your control? Possibly, but striving to maintain that "ideal" woman's weight (or men's, for that matter) can carry with it a degree of physical and mental injury. You decide.

Chapter 21: Questioning the Truth That "Body Language" Tells All

The idea that how we position parts of our body, our facial movements, and even the direction we turn when speaking reveals the truth about everything about us has been around since Ray Birdwhistell, an anthropologist, proposed body language. He wasn't the only one interested in this phenomenon because Albert Mehrabian, too, found it revealing.

One thing needs to be made clear here, and that is the difference between a theory and a hypothesis. Theories are based on scientific facts that result from stringent experimentation, while hypotheses are assumptions yet to be proven and not based on scientific facts; if they were, they'd be theories.

Unquestionably, having insight into what motivates someone, how they are feeling emotionally, or whether they are attempting to deceive us would be an important skill, and body language has been seen as that inroad to the unconscious. But not always, and here is where we must consider the mental state of the individual in question.

According to research, individuals who suffer from bipolar disorder (BD), as well as those who suffer from autism spectrum disorders or schizophrenia (among other types of psychopathology), frequently exhibit deficiencies in social cognition that have a detrimental effect on their relationships and their quality of life. Body language in their cases may be quite faulty at best.

But that leaves out those with personality disorders who may have developed a means to avoid detection—or can they? Do their bodies still betray them and send messages they don't want to be seen? We do know about the lying brain, don't we? And then there are what are referred to in poker as "tells." These are small, mostly unconscious, moves that let the other players know what the player is considering or if he's holding a winning hand. Why do you suppose some of them wear sunglasses while playing?

Research has produced some interesting results with people who are not police officers (yes, they are better at this). When people try to tell the difference between lies and truths in real time, without any special tools or training, they get 54% of the time right, correctly identifying 47% of lies as false and 61% of truths as true.

What's a coin toss chance of getting something right? Fifty percent of the time? So, it's a bit better than this. But there may be one area of the body that holds a host of significant signs regarding attempts to lie or tell the truth, and they are mixed and not always what we believe.

But is body language universal and can we use it in other cultures? Some body movements and gestures are unique to certain cultures. However, it is worth looking into whether more subtle nonverbal communication gestures are understood by people from all backgrounds. Birdwhistell did not think that there were universals in human behavior when it came to body language, but research by Dr. Paul Ekman showed that there are some similarities between cultures.

Attempting to bring science to body language, or at least in terms of facial expressions, has resulted in the Facial Action Coding System. The FACS is responsible for computer encoding the movements of individual facial muscles based on the minor variations in face appearance that occur from moment to moment. Both animators and psychologists have used it.

Another software program that can be used to monitor facial expressions for a variety of purposes is Facial Expression Analysis. The website for this computerized module notes, "*While no single sensor is able to read minds, the synthesis of multiple data streams combined with strong empirical methods can begin to reach in that direction.*" They further indicate its uses:

1. Measure personality correlates of facial behavior

2. Test affective dynamics in game-based learning

3. Explore emotional responses in teaching simulations

4. Assessing physiological responses to driving in different conditions

The company indicates it's for use with academics but does not list on their website the studies used to verify their results.

But body language isn't restricted to humans; it is reaching into the animal domain to see what various postures or expressions mean. One area is now receiving interest because of an increase in raising alpacas and how their actions can be interpreted.

An accurate understanding of these animals' behavior makes sure they are raised and used in a way that meets their needs, improves their health, and helps people build a positive relationship with alpacas. In one internet study, people who had degrees in agricultural sciences, forestry, or veterinary sciences were better at recognizing the signals that the alpacas were sending in the pictures presented to them than people who had degrees in biological sciences or other fields.

Previous research has indicated that when dealing with many types of animals, like horses, alpacas, cattle, and dogs, you should pay attention to where the ears, head, and tail are. There seems to be evidence for their body language, and, in terms of dogs, this is particularly important when they are interacting with children.

Is body language sufficiently scientific? It may not meet all the criteria, but it appears to be useful in multiple situations across cultures and even with animals.

Chapter 22: Hunger and Weight Control and an Eye-Opening Discovery

The battle against unwanted weight causes untold misery for far too many, and the standard advice is lifestyle changes, exercise, and caloric restriction, for the most part. Aside from subscribing to highly expensive weight-loss medications (about $1,000/mo.) for untold months of life or expensive food plans, there seems to be little else to do.

But the body is still holding fast to its mysteries, and we've only recently, in the past decade, begun to explore weight, or, in particular, taste and our weight. Vision, too, can be added to the equation, but that's not been explored too much. Food display is very important in tempting us to try foods, isn't it?

We've been told there may be something akin to an addiction to fast foods or taste, especially regarding sweetness or saltiness, and we should avoid those foods. Yes, it's good advice, but there's even more to know about weight, and it can be a very surprising revelation for consumers and healthcare professionals alike.

Where do you think our sense of taste lies in our bodies? Probably all of us will say it's those all-important taste buds on our tongue, right? Well, Mother Nature didn't design us that way, and that's a myth that has been thrown in the dumpster. Penn and Teller weren't needed, and researchers went alone on their relentless journeys. They proved it to be just that—a myth—with the discovery of T2R receptors.

Research has discovered that the brain has a hunger or satiety structure, the hypothalamus. We've known that for years, but now taste receptors have been found in the heart. Although the details remain unclear, it does seem taste receptors have some physiologic relevance as metabolite and nutrient sensors in the heart.

It is essential for life that the heart work properly and continuously. Finding T2Rs in heart cells suggests that they play important (but not fully understood) roles in heart physiology and how it reacts to outside factors like diet, metabolic changes, infections, and drugs.

It is hard to do research, however, and learn about the physiology of T2Rs in the human heart because it is hard to get suitable human heart tissue, and the work has been done with lab rats. Of course, we have to question if there is sufficient validity for this finding between rats and human hearts.

Taste is an important part of our functioning since it can alert us to dangers, such as when food is spoiled or has an unusual and unfamiliar taste. The body has sensors for all of that. About 29 bitter taste receptors (T2Rs) are found in the human genome. These receptors can pick up on thousands of bitter ligands, such as harmful and unpleasant chemicals.

How the heart's taste receptors may act on weight control and how the drugs used to control weight may, similarly, affect these cardiac receptors remains a secret to be unlocked with more research. But the more we learn, the more we understand how complex weight and its control may be.

Chapter Twenty-Three

Chapter 23: Anxiety Disorders Have a New Addition, and It's Fed by the Internet

A nxiety disorders are common, and there are at least 20 discrete anxiety disorders listed in the DSM-5 published by the American Psychiatric Association. However, even though there are separate disorders, anxiety is usually included as a factor in other disorders, such as depression.

The popularity of the internet, with its vast trove of information, often aided by algorithms such as ChatGPT, has become the next information-heavy wave when searching for medical information. Does anyone remember when people in the healthcare profession scoffed at "Dr. Google" when patients indicated they had found relevant information regarding their symptoms? The ease of symptom searching for those with a more-than-usual interest in their medical health has led to the designation of yet another anxiety-related disorder.

Cyberchondria is when someone searches for health information online over and over again, which causes them to feel more anxious and distressed about their health. It is a multifaceted construct known as a "transdiagnostic compulsive behavioral syndrome" that is associated with three elements: obsessive-compulsive symptoms, problematic internet use, and anxiety-related factors.

There is not a single agreed-upon definition of cyberchondria, but most of them focus on online health research that is linked to higher levels of distress or anxiety. The two main theories of cyberchondria are based on reassurance-seeking and certain metacognitive beliefs. Any significant health outbreak, such as the COVID-19 pandemic, may fuel the disorder, which has implications for public health in terms of impaired functioning and changes in healthcare utilization.

It is also important to think about how much the condition might be like a behavioral addiction as a form of problematic internet use. Cyberchondria may have become more common during the COVID-19 pandemic, with people who are more likely to have health-related anxiety being more likely to experience it. Some data supports the idea that cyberchondria might be a behavioral addiction, but there are still many things we do not fully understand.

A study surveying patients at health clinics found reasons for concern regarding health anxiety. Out of the 43,205 people who went to the clinics, 28,991 (67.1%) were evaluated, and of those left over after patients who were not qualified were taken out, 5,747 (19.8%) had significant health anxiety. The researchers concluded that abnormal health anxiety, which is prevalent and a major concern among those who visit medical clinics, is something that should receive more attention.

If we look simply at hypochondriasis without adding cyberchondria, the concern for health and life mounts. A study in Sweden looked at 4,129 people who had been diagnosed with hypochondriasis and 41,290 demographically similar people who did not have hypochondriasis. The people who did have hypochondriasis had a higher chance of dying from both natural and unnatural causes, especially suicide.

One major issue is that those with the disorder may avoid medical attention altogether, and the results may be dire. A Norwegian longitudinal cohort study of 7,052 people found that after 12 years, people who said they had symptoms of health anxiety were 73% more likely to develop ischemic heart disease than people who said they did not have any symptoms of health anxiety. Was it anxiety that brought it on or the avoidance of medical evaluation that led to its development?

In a different study, people who felt more health anxiety after looking for medical information on the Internet reported more PIU (problematic Internet use) than people whose health anxiety did not change after searching for medical information or went down after searching.

Lifetime rates of health anxiety are 6% in the general population and as high as 20% in hospital outpatients. This causes more medical visits that are unnecessary, which costs the health system more money. Rates for healthcare may be rising because more people are browsing the internet excessively (cyberchondria) and requesting more assessments.

What can be done to help these individuals in terms of healthcare treatments? Some people find that antidepressants help with health anxiety, but they do not like taking them. On the other hand, cognitive behavior therapy, stress management, mindfulness training, and acceptance and commitment therapy have all been shown to be helpful in the short and long term. These therapies can be given one-on-one, in groups, or over the Internet.

The bottom line is that we may have a new addiction to put into any forthcoming DSM, or it may be placed in the area where it is of concern and needs more investigation. But, in the meantime, individuals who find they are avoiding medical evaluations and ceaselessly searching the internet for help should consider mental health treatment for their anxiety.

Chapter 24: Green Space Is Associated with Something Extraordinary — Kids' Bone Strength

G reen space is receiving more attention for its environmental
benefits, how it nourishes the land, its insects, and the entire

biosphere on which we depend. But other aspects of green space have been passed by and now we're beginning to tap into additional and essential aspects of it in terms of physical health even before birth.

Studies have found that having more green space during pregnancy is linked to higher birth weight and a lower risk of low birth weight (LBW). Also, having more green space as a child was linked to more physical activity and a lower risk of obesity and neurodevelopmental problems such as not paying attention.

A study of kids ages 4 to 6 found that children who spent more time in residential green spaces had higher bone mineral density and a lower risk of having low bone density. These results show how important it is to be exposed to residential green spaces early in life for bone health during important times of growth and development, which can have long-lasting effects. But how does green space contribute to this change? Fractures appear to be a common occurrence in children. How might the two be related?

For kids in the U.S., falls are the main reason they go to the emergency room (ED) with injuries. Children between 5 to 9 accounted for 38% of the unintentional fall injuries in 2021, and falls were the main cause of their injuries, accounting for about 14% of all pediatric injury-related ED visits in 2010.

Two-thirds of all fractures in children happen in the upper limbs, and the most common type of fracture in both boys and girls is the forearm. Additionally, depending on the type of fracture, children may be limited in their free time activities for a certain number of days. This may be necessary but can contribute to other psychological problems for the child.

New research is giving rise to an increased interest in the investigation regarding what might account for kids' fractures and how to strengthen their bones to decrease fracture incidence. The solution appears to be a simple one: green spaces. But if you consider that simplistically, you'd be wrong.

The latest research is gradually uncovering what scientists believe are some of the factors related to children's bone density. One study looked at 327 children between the ages of 4 and 6 years old. Those who lived in areas with more green space had significantly higher bone mineral density. Additionally, areas with more green space within a 1000-m radius were significantly linked with lower odds of having low bone density.

We know that peak bone mass is reached in early adulthood and depends on how much bone mass is gained during skeletal growth and development. Because of this, not getting enough bone mass at a young age is just as important for developing osteoporosis as losing bone mass as you age. Therefore, focusing on increasing bone mass in the early stages of life may lower the risk of fractures and/or osteoporosis later on.

The latest children's bone density findings point to factors we would normally associate with the availability of green space, and it's not the vegetation but the space available for kids and adults. The number of accessible green spaces close to home, their safety, and the variety of natural and social facilities all affect how people use green spaces.

Because of the space surrounding their homes, it seems likely that participants in this study would have walked from home to the closest available and accessible green space (like a park, garden, or forest) close by. They would, therefore, engage in a range of physically taxing activities that would encourage bone strength, whereas sitting before a computer screen or playing video games would have little benefit.

However, we can assume that there are also sociocultural factors involved here. What group would more likely have access to green space?

Who lives in housing that minimizes the green spaces in the area, and what children have parents with higher socioeconomic status? We can be talking about societal privilege and not green space at all.

The research makes strong, obscured statements regarding architectural design that incorporates green spaces not as attractive landscaping features but as health-promoting housing that reaches far into the children's futures. How many of the reviews of this latest "finding" also provide space for consideration of how some kids develop stronger bones and go on to be healthier adults, while others will develop a greater need for healthcare as adults?

Chapter 25: Ableism Is a Hindrance for the Mobility Challenged, But Who Cares?

Anyone who walks around any city, anywhere in the world, never has to consider how they will get from one place to another. These are the individuals who are now involved in ableism or being able-bodied. But those with mobility issues have to solve that problem for every trip they make, every vacation they'd like to go on, or any park, building, market, or school they might want to visit. And they have to contend with the ableists they will encounter on any trip. Using a wheelchair changes how people see a person right away and in a big way.

I once asked someone responsible for a birdwatching park about the paths or boardwalks. He said all paths were gravel, and the entrance to one area was behind a large shopping mall in the area. Quickly, he tried to reassure me that anyone with a walker or wheelchair could use the paths. He had no idea how difficult it might be to use a wheelchair or rolling walker on gravel. As for lavatories, he said they were no longer available to anyone.

Leaving home or an apartment for those with mobility issues isn't simply locking the door, hopping into the car, or jumping on a bike. Wouldn't it be wonderful if all everyone had to do was as simple as that? Those with mobility issues aren't free from the physical impediments that make any travel a well-planned activity beforehand. Some places may be out of bounds, either because of the architecture or the geology of particular places, and that is limiting.

The Spanish Steps? Most people know that famous spot in Rome, Italy, but if you're using a walker or a wheelchair, how do you navigate that? In New York City, there is a well-known place called the Joker Stairs in the Bronx that was featured in a film. Again, there's no way everyone who might want to experience this classic feature can. But these are exaggerations, right? How about any neighborhood in your area?

But a new time is coming because, recently, I heard of an out-of-town law firm that has found a lucrative trove of suits to file for ADA violations by stores and restaurants. One store paid the firm $20K to not file a case against them. Does it take lawsuits to correct this discrimination? But everyone with a disability CAN file an action.

According to traditional beliefs, medicine is a kind field where every person's life is valued equally, and there is no bias or discrimination. Although this may still be the ideal that medicine aspires to, the reality is that how society generally perceives and treats individuals and groups that are considered to be "others" still has an impact on medical professionals.

In the past year, I have accompanied someone to medical appointments. The woman uses a rolling walker and finds it difficult, almost impossible, to pull herself up onto an exam table. But shouldn't a medical office have at least one lower exam table for those who need it?

Another medical office does have a lower exam table, but only one, and if it's in use, there is no option. In that case, she is examined while seated in a straight-backed chair. Is that sufficient for an exam? Is that what they teach is permissible in medical school?

I was once interviewing a woman who had MS and needed to use a walker. One problem she had was "handicapped parking" (now called "disability parking"). The market had at least four spots allocated for cars with the requisite placards, "but they're halfway across the parking lot from the store's entrance," she told me. Anyone familiar with the ADA regulations would know that both the parking spots and any store's entrance and exit must be the shortest distance away from each other.

In addition to the location of the spots and the building entrance, there are other regulations.

Car-accessible spaces must:

    1. Be at least 96 inches wide

2. Have an access aisle at least 60 inches wide

3. Have no more than a 1.48 (2.08%) slope in all directions

4. Have a surface that is firm, stable, and slip-resistant

5. Have a sign with the international symbol of accessibility on it, mounted at least 60 inches above the ground (measured to the bottom of the sign)

Then there's the part about entrances. *"In parking lots or garages, accessible parking spaces must be located on the shortest accessible route to the accessible entrance. An accessible route is the path a person with a disability takes to enter and move through a building or facility."*

And this is only the parking portion of the ADA. What about door openers, interior spaces with ramps, lavatories, etc.?

No one needs to be a psychology major to understand how ableism affects those with disabilities. One activist has coined a term that relates to it well. Inspiring tales about disabilities are associated with the term "inspiration porn," which activist Stella Young coined. Inspiration porn is described as "objectifying disabled people for the benefit of nondisabled people."

Schools have tried sensitivity training with students. Padding, special shoes, eyeshades, and other materials are intended to mimic some physical impairment of mobility or vision, but we have to wonder how effective these charades play out in the real world.

Try a test for yourself in terms of your ableism and understanding of disability. Borrow a walker (not the one with wheels) and walk around your main street, where all the stores are located. Use the walker as a disabled person. No picking it up and walking. Place it down for each step.

Pick a few stores and try to open the doors while still standing within the protective curved area of the walker. What about going up and down off the sidewalk into the roadway and crossing the street? How long did it take to get across the street, and what about the traffic?

How are people looking at or relating to you? Is it somehow different? Did you find any of it difficult?

Anyone desiring additional information regarding laws, organizations, or other matters has access to a wealth of resources via the Internet.

ADA.gov

ADA Guidance & Resource Materials

ADA Information Line

US Dept. of Education

US Dept. of Labor

US General Services Administration

Library of Congress

Chapter 26: The Debunked Test That Can Upset Your Career Options

E very year, about 80 million people take personality tests. The industry is expected to grow to $6.5 billion by 2027, and 80% of Fortune 500 companies use personality tests to hire people. However, personality tests are based on the idea that traits are fixed, which can have an unfair effect on candidates.

Several companies have been charged with discrimination for using personality tests. Strengths-based leadership is a better way to build a successful team. Companies have used tests despite not knowing their limitations.

One of the most potentially harmful of these tests, and one of the most widely used in corporate America, is the M**yers-Briggs Test**, a test that many have found flawed, inaccurate, and based on pseudo-science. How can it be that a test that is essentially useless in what it purports to do is still seen as the one to trust the most in hiring?

We could say it's an undeserved preeminence in testing without earning it, laziness on the part of corporate HR people, poor policy, and a host of other factors. But the one factor that matters is that it shouldn't be used, and it can ruin prospective employees' efforts to build their careers by short-cutting their options.

Most of the research that supports the MBTI was done by the Center for Applications of Psychological Type, which is run by the Myers-Briggs Foundation. The research was then published in the center's own journal, the Journal of Psychological Type (JPT), which brings up issues of independence, bias, and conflict of interest. How many people who use this scale in HR are familiar with the construction and inherent problems with this instrument?

Katharine Briggs, who had no formal training in psychology, was inspired by the psychological concepts of Carl Jung and started by testing the personalities of neighborhood kids in her living room. She wanted to come up with educational plans that would help each child reach their full potential. To do this, she gave the kids' parents a forced-choice questionnaire that had only two possible answers (A or B). It asked parents things like, "Is your child calm or impulsive? Do they do things that make you happy or sad?"

She was very religious and thought that the only way to save your soul was to discover who you were and live your life in line with your best self. It's not a bad idea, even if you don't believe in the concept of having a soul and her religious bent.

Her daughter, Isabel, constructed a questionnaire from her mother's work. The 93-question test says it can divide all people into 16 distinct "types," which can then be used as a framework for building better relationships, driving positive change, harnessing innovation, and achieving excellence. Most people who take it see it mainly as a way to find out what career they should go into.

Once WWII began, a frantic search by recruitment agencies began, and they hit upon the Myers-Briggs as the instrument that answered their needs. From there, universities, seeing that the government was using the test, began using it for admissions. Then corporations saw it as a means of weeding out potential employees, and its legend grew, but not its validity.

In the first place, the entire thesis of this hypothesis about personality was never intended as a questionnaire for anything. It was a means to immerse yourself in Jungian thinking and, over the years, help yourself in your life, not corporate employment. But Myers' daughter had a different view, devised the questionnaire, and went on to "fame."

From the living room to corporate settings, the test has now embedded itself in America's employment efforts and *has yet to be proven valid.* Even Jung's hypotheses have not been scientifically tested and remain interesting thoughts on human behavior.

It was an era of initiative in psychology, where it was attempting to prove itself as a science, and we are living with the results of those efforts, which remain problematic. But the test goes on in corporate America, earning an *estimated $20 million yearly or more.*

Chapter 27: Charity in an Era of Constantly Requesting Donations

C haritable giving, whether money, clothing, household necessi-
ties, or food, in addition to other items, is good for our mental
health, and scientists have shown this to be true. We gain as others do,
and that's a good thing, but not when we are constantly bombarded
by requests from organizations, political causes, or politicians.

Not simply the stress is at work here, but the whole question of to
whom we should give and how that tears at our emotions to give to

some and not to others. Making the choice isn't easy when it comes to kids with cancer, working to protect our democracy, or helping starving people, hungry children, or abused animals. All of them use the same tactic: our sense of empathy, altruism, and morality.

The TV ads are extremely clever and heartbreaking, especially when we see the carefully chosen graphics that make it all the more stressful. Watching a child with their parents in activities where they have no mask or tubes attached and then being hit in the gut with the fact that they're dead is bordering on the cruel.

One of my main concerns about advertising and charitable giving has been the extraordinary amount of money invested in TV ads. How much of our contributions actually go to the programs, and how much is used for agency fees or executive salaries? I recall years ago a mini-backlash when it was found that a children's charity was spending inordinate funds on executive salaries, not kids in need. So, what do we do, and where do we go?

One place to research charities is **Charity Navigator,** which provides ratings on charitable organizations. They also have a Best Charities by Cause section where you can drill down on where you want to make donations. Or, you can support Empower the Underdog, a charity that needs more funding.

Avoid charity scams, too. I occasionally get a phone call from an organization claiming to help disabled police officers or firefighters. One fool, and they always have deep, masculine voices, said I had made a contribution from my office on a certain day. I told him that it was a Sunday and I was never in the office, and I hung up. They still try the scam once or twice a year. BTW, NEVER OPEN attachments to charitable solicitations.

What about executive compensation for non-profits? Here's one that really hurts. Then you might want to look at **Charity Watch,** where they filter out the facts from the ad and compensation donations. Take a look at the executive compensation packages for major charities. Here are their ratings on a number of charities.

The holidays are prime time for all charities and scams, so think wisely before you pull out that credit card or send in that check. Here are their top-rated charities by category.

Being charitable is good for everyone, but the scammers are out there waiting for us and devising new ways to get our money; beware.

Chapter 28: Psychedelics for Mental Health Care: Unexpected Uses

H ealthcare research appears to be re-evaluating what Timothy Leary was always preaching regarding "street drugs": turn on, tune in, drop out. A Harvard University clinical psychologist, Leary began studying the use of psychotropic drugs and their effects on the mind.

Richard Alpert and Leary started the **Harvard Psilocybin Project** to find out how it affected people's minds by giving it to volunteers (who were not fully informed about the drug's actions) and recording their real-time accounts of the experience. During the time that Leary and Alpert were doing research at Harvard, neither LSD nor psilocybin was illegal in the United States. Harvard's concerns, however, were raised and compounded because the project was poorly designed, and both researchers were under the influence of the drug during the experiments.

A 34-year follow-up study showed that the published claims that Leary's experiments had a treatment effect were incorrect. This second study, however, backs up the original reports' emphasis on how important it is to include psilocybin-assisted psychotherapy with prisoners as part of a full treatment plan that includes nondrug group support programs after they get out of jail.

Leary was viewed as somewhat of a maverick in the academic community because of his espousal of psychedelics as a means of "mind-broadening" our daily experiences. But as we've seen in the coming rescheduling of marijuana by the FDA from Schedule 1 to Schedule 3 and changes in laws to permit marijuana shops for consumers to open, there is more change coming.

The thinking now is that drugs such as psilocybin and MDMA have the ability to change individual brain cells, can assist in the rewiring of the brain, and may provide a novel approach to the treatment of a wide range of conditions, including chronic pain and depression.

To determine the efficacy and safety of psychedelic drug treatment, academic medical centers in the United States are conducting clinical trials. These trials are using drugs that are either prohibited or severely restricted for therapeutic use. They include psilocybin, which is an ingredient in "magic mushrooms," MDMA (3,4-methylenedioxy-methamphetamine, also known by its street name, ecstasy), LSD, and ketamine.

The trials are intended to treat a variety of mental health conditions, including post-traumatic stress disorder (PTSD), depression, addiction to drugs and alcohol, smoking, eating disorders, prolonged grief, cluster headaches, and burnout among healthcare workers.

Anyone wishing to investigate clinical trial availability for any drug or illness and wishing for information can access the *National Library of Medicine's Clinical Trials* searchable database. One thing to remember, however, is that this research is ongoing, which means that much of it may not be replicated and is still called into question regarding its usefulness in mental health disorders. Because these substances are being used in clinical trials, does not mean that they are safe for anyone to use at home, and it should not be assumed that this article is recommending that to anyone.

Chapter 29: When the Wonderful Weight-Loss Drugs Stop Working, Then What?

N ote on weight-loss drugs: More than fifty lawsuits say that
Novo Nordisk or Eli Lilly did not tell patients about the bad

effects of their famous diabetes or weight loss drugs. Some of these medicines are Ozempic, Wegovy, and Rybelsus from Novo Nordisk and Trulicity and Mounjaro from Eli Lilly. The same federal judge in Philadelphia is handling all of these personal injury claims because they all involve the same class of drugs.

Studies have shown that people who stop taking these weight-loss drugs—either because they want to or because they can get them—gain back most of the weight they lost, if not all of it. This is not unusual, since we've seen other medications reach a point where they lose the efficacy they once had and "poop out" as healthcare professionals say.

What is even more frustrating with weight-loss drugs is that people who keep taking them (some at $1,000 a month) eventually reach a plateau where their bodies do not seem to lose any more weight. At this point, the complete action of the drugs, according to some experts, isn't known, but we do know that the body, in some mysterious way, has a set point and that's where it stops drugs from working.

But doctors say some people seek out these drugs to lose as much weight as possible — and are dismayed and disillusioned when they stop. Some go off the drugs after they hit their plateau. When they do, they tend to regain the weight they lost.

Ozempic and similar medications work by simulating a hormone that the body produces, which in turn slows the stomach's emptying rate, making us feel fuller for longer. Additionally, they reduce cravings by acting on the parts of the brain that control hunger. The precise mechanisms by which they operate remain unclear, however, and this includes the reasons why some people reach a plateau at a particular weight.

Perhaps it's an innate means of protection that we have that remains to be properly studied. Some call it a form of physical self-regulation that the body imposes.

In the short term, you may lose weight because your metabolism slows down. This means that your body needs less energy to do the same things, so the food you eat does not burn as quickly. You may start gaining weight again. Your body may also attempt to get you back to your same weight as before by changing hormone levels that affect your appetite and metabolism. It may also change the amount of water you drink. The process is both fascinating and formidable, plus it causes a lot of frustration for the person who wants to lose weight.

People stop taking the drugs voluntarily because of the side effects that were noticed when these medications were initially used for Type 2 diabetic patients. The most common reasons given by doctors (n = 443) for patients stopping GLP-1 medications were that patients were unable to control blood sugar well (45.6%), felt sick or were throwing up (43.8%), had gut (GI) side effects (36.8%), and there were other side effects like constipation or diarrhea. The patients stopped because they preferred oral medications over injectable ones.

One investigation found that the average yearly cost of care for people before they started taking Wegovy or a similar drug was $12,371. After they started taking the drug, the average cost of care rose by 59% to $19,657 per year. How many non-diabetic patients, or, for that matter, anyone, can afford almost $20,000 a year to lose weight? Not all health insurance plans will pay for these treatments. And recall that these individuals will have to take these drugs for the rest of their lives. It's not a one-shot-and-done deal.

Weight loss drugs (like Wegovy or Zepbound) or diabetes drugs (like Ozempic or Mounjaro), when you stop taking them, they all have the same side effects.

Some possible side effects of stopping weight loss drugs are:

Return or growth in hunger

Different amounts of sugar in the blood

Gain weight again

Because these medicines may make your stomach upset, you may also notice that your diarrhea, nausea, or other side effects go away after you stop taking them.

Consistency is the most important thing for weight loss, no matter if you are changing your diet, working out more, taking prescription drugs, or having surgery. Even bariatric surgery may not permanently keep the weight off. A colleague at a college where I once taught went for bariatric surgery and lost over 100 lbs., but within two years he gained it all back.

Another experience provided me with an unusual look at a diet doctor's office. I went with a friend who was a patient of this diet specialist in an upscale neighborhood. The women sitting in the waiting room averaged over 400 lbs., some more, and they all waited for their plexiglass boxes to be filled for the week, to be weighed, and then they left. What was in the carefully portioned-off boxes? Several pills were in each section, but one, I believe called "black beauties," was in there too. The women were taking amphetamines unknowingly.

The women never saw the physician, only the receptionist who checked and refilled their boxes, and the other person, who I assumed was a nurse, who weighed them, took their pulse and blood pressure, and bid them goodbye until the next week.

The key to weight loss isn't a quick fix or a see-through box; it's staying consistent and changing your habits. If Wegovy or Ozempic are chosen, then people should know they have to take those drugs for life to keep off the weight. How many of those taking these medications now know that fact?

When they're no longer working or if they lose their job or retire, they'll still have to take the drugs to keep the weight off. Will they be able to afford it, and do they know about the set point in weight?

People in the entertainment field can, I would assume, write these drugs off as expenses for taxes and the price of keeping their jobs or getting contracts. How many of us need to take these very expensive drugs to keep our jobs? I would suspect there are very few fields where that would be the case outside of the entertainment fields.

How many people give in to the influence of well-known female stars or personalities who promote diet plans, food plans, gym memberships, or equipment plans? Do they know those women can all have their diet-conscious chefs and plastic surgeons to keep them trim and young-looking? It's not the tiny saucer-size spaghetti that does it for them.

Know how Mario Lanza, the man with an incredible voice comparable to that of Enrico Caruso died? The media had reported he went to a clinic in Europe, where they used a radical treatment originally thought to be useful in childbirth, to lose weight and only be fed intravenously. What happened? He died there.

There are also people whose body types will always be fuller than the cultural standard being pitched at them. They will have a genetically determined body weight, fuller breasts, and wider hips. Should they be ashamed of who they are and where they came from? Nature didn't make all of us out of one mold. Some of us were genetically sized for the climate where we live, and others for factors unknown to us.

We have to wonder if these drugs are the answer to the prayers of millions who are shamed and discriminated against because of their weight. There's nothing humorous about being overweight, especially when too many people feel it's acceptable to be cruel or to make fun of anyone who is obese. Even the word "obese" is stigmatizing. Certainly, the TV producers have jumped on the bandwagon. I won't mention the shows, but I find them inordinately cruel.

One additional note about some of the weight loss drugs is needed here. Since they were introduced, some adverse reactions have been noted, such as **vision difficulties** in some of them and **extreme nausea** in others. In addition, long-term use may result in *increased blood pressure and heart rate, insomnia, nervousness, restlessness, dependence, abuse or withdrawal.*

Chapter 30: Spare Us from the Tyranny of the BMI in Weight Determination

The BMI is treated with kid gloves as though it deserves some revered place in healthcare and is the golden standard for determining whether or not someone is obese. While it may be used universally for that purpose, its past and its design leave much to be desired.

Concern about being overweight (defined as a body mass index [BMI] of 30 or higher is taken very seriously, which is surprising given its history. Fear of being overweight did not start as a medical issue. It took off in the mid-18th century when some race scientists started saying that being "too fat" was bad because it was linked to women of color.

In the 20th century, the search for a useful measure of relative body weight began after actuaries reported that their overweight clients were more likely to die. It reached its peak after World War II when studies looked into the link between weight and cardiovascular disease. So, it wasn't a medical quest at all, but one based originally on outlaying money for consumers with poor health and using too much healthcare.

Adolphe Quetelet (1796–1874) was a Belgian mathematician who calculated the original form of today's BMI when he determined that while babies and teenagers grow quickly at first, "the weight increases as the square of the height." This was called the Quetelet Index until Ancel Keys (1904–2004) changed it to the Body Mass Index. It had its roots in skewed thinking regarding race and culture.

Eugenics, too, played a central role in weight determination and what it indicated about the individual. Charles Davenport, a zoologist, said that being overweight was a defect in the human race. The "low" types showed this way of being, with Chinese and Jewish people being more likely to experience racial obesity. Where's the medical science here?

The BMI does not accurately reflect overweight and obesity, whether it is based on self-reported weight and height or recorded weight and height. It is thought to be better to measure total body fat because it gives an idea of whether the body is mostly fat or mostly lean. Unfortunately, this is hard to measure in clinical practice, so it cannot be used in regular care. However, it has been shown that BMI is not very good at either sensitivity or precision.

How does the BMI fail in its intended objective? BMI was created based on white males and does not apply to people of other races or ethnicities. Experts have also said that BMI does not take into account things like how much fat a person has compared to muscle, where their fat is distributed in their body (usually, fat around the waist raises disease risk more than fat in other places), or their metabolic health. Looking back at the original calculations, we can quickly see that it fails in terms of age, body type, and other features of body type and weight. It's a flawed metric.

A subtle groundswell is being raised regarding discarding the BMI as a superior measure for assessing questions related to weight, whether healthy or otherwise. This unreliable measure is often part of electronic health records. Payors and quality-improvement policies at clinics or hospitals encourage physicians to check, categorize, and act on BMI at most encounters.

Research has also shown that using BMI as a health indicator can lead to misdiagnosis, patient dissatisfaction, stigmatization, and failure to follow through on proper healthcare. Patients whose BMI is "normal" but who are cardiometabolically unhealthy are ignored—about 30% of this population. The estimate in one article was that 74,936,678 people are misclassified when BMI is used as the main measure of cardiometabolic health. If doctors think these people are "healthy" just because they are not overweight or obese, important diagnoses could be delayed or missed.

If the measure is not valid, how can anyone support its use for such vital medical issues? It doesn't stand to reason that any other flawed measure would be used in other situations, so why the BMI? Because that's what they've always used. No, BMI should not be the default when it comes to weight-related matters.

What should be done if healthcare professionals don't see the BMI as the be-all-and-end-all metric? There is at least one change in the medical evaluation of a patient. Before a patient is weighed, the practitioner needs to ask themselves two simple questions: Is BMI necessary for making medical decisions at this time? Could focusing on weight be providing this patient care or making them feel bad about themselves?

It's not all weight and BMI, and a degree of psychological awareness is needed before entering into any assessment. But there may also be a new way to best assess weight and all the factors that enter into health and that would be the power of AI and an algorithm that might be devised.

Chapter 31: Questioning Seclusion, Isolation and Solitary Confinement

Transgender individuals who are sent to prisons are punished in ways too ugly for us to imagine. Simple criminal offenses do not give the right to any facility to sexually abuse, isolate or terrorize someone in any way. Our criminal justice system is supposed to mean responsible rehabilitation, but I doubt that happens as we would wish. Instead, through the force of brutality, whether by guards or inmates, they come out more damaged than when they went in. Haven't we done a wonderful job here? Shouldn't we celebrate our success in breaking the spirit, if not the souls, of those individuals? Ask yourself how you reacted to the recent news about the culture of violence against young inmates at one of New York City's jails, Rikers Island. Did you read about it? What did you do?

Today, the issue of transgender inmates gained prominence, and the situation was far worse than anyone could have predicted. Because of their special status, they are put into a form of housing that makes brutality even more possible. How do we protect someone when they are in isolation for 23 hours a day and guards act as though they were their personal playthings? True, being a prison guard can bring out the worst in some individuals, especially if the guards' culture is a festering pool of ignorance and violence. Who should be locked up here?

The guards on Rikers seemingly acted with impunity because no one believed the inmates or held the guards accountable for their crimes. What's going to be done now? I'm a firm believer in unions, but I hope their union doesn't jump to protect the brutes who abused the inmates because that's what labor organizations sometimes do. As a matter of fact, I was once an elected union official, so I am not to be sluffed off as a no-nothing do-gooder.

However, jails are not the only places that allow evil to flourish. Psychiatric hospitals and any other facility that enjoys a significant degree of privacy can also serve as prime hotspots. Have you ever feared being admitted to a psychiatric facility? The portrayals we've seen in the media and films (think "The Snake Pit" or even "Cuckoo's Nest" or "Titicut Follies") and you get the idea quickly. Does it happen anymore? I think it very well might, but let me tell you something I heard about. It didn't happen within the past few years, but the individuals involved are probably still in their positions of authority because it pays so well and they do so little work.

A young man in a psychiatric hospital went to the ward staff in great distress. He said he was being raped nightly by another male patient on the unit. Did they believe him? Not really, but it was reported, and they had to do something because someone made a chart notes, and those are reviewed by JCAHO (Joint Commission on Accreditation of Healthcare Organizations), and that means funding, friends. When money is involved, action takes place.

The in-house patient advocate didn't seem capable of marshaling an adequate defense for this young man, but an outside advocate did just that. She was a member of a group appointed by her state to monitor care of patients in these facilities, and she wanted a review. Prior to the review, ward staff handled the matter by providing the man with a powerful sleep-inducing medication each evening and locking him in a seclusion room. The room had little more than a thin foam mattress on the floor, but at least he felt safe. But how do you justify putting a patient in seclusion each night? You really can't do it without a review by a psychiatrist.

The team met and the outside advocate was there, the facility's medical director, responsible ward staff, the unit psychiatrist and the ward physician. The chart was reviewed, and the ward physician was instructed by the medical director to do a physical examination of the young man to determine if he was being raped. Notes were taken, and everyone left. Did the ward physician do the exam? I never heard he did. What happened to the young man? He was likely transferred to a different unit where he might encounter similar indifferent staff behavior.

Seclusion, as I've seen, is at the whim of whoever is in charge, and it's a rather simple matter for staff to precipitate an incident if they are so inclined. I would think this happens in jails, nursing homes and juvenile detention facilities, too. Push a patient or an inmate far enough, know what their "buttons" are, and you get what you want: punishment for them. Nursing homes that wanted to dump problem patients would not give them their psychiatric meds. Result? They acted out and were transferred to a psychiatric hospital. When it came time to return them to the nursing home, the home refused to take them. Result? One more psychiatric patient, one less in the nursing home.

So, don't just look at prisons. Look at every facility where anyone is housed either temporarily or permanently and hold everyone accountable for their actions. I was once warned by a head nurse that if I were to report something, I could expect that my car would be keyed or worse. I've heard of staff loosening the lug nuts on someone's car or flattening all four tires. It's criminal behavior, and it's done by hospital staff. No, let's not just say "hospital staff" because I'm sure it happens at other facilities, too.

All of us need to be aware of the problems and the possible remedies and hold everyone accountable for their actions.

Chapter 32: The Woody Allen Cover That Wasn't

Memories are wonderful things, except when they bring back those "almost" things. The things that almost happened but didn't and you wonder why; you try to explain it, to understand it and then you hit the wall of trying and just accept. It was an almost, and now it's a curious memory.

Watching a Woody Allen film, "Hollywood Ending," it came back to me as though it had happened not that long ago, but is was another age in my life. I am constantly reading about writers and getting offers of seminars, quick writing tips and software or TED programs that will bring back or jog my creativity into overdrive. Not just get me going on creativity, but really steamrolling along.

It's the same with everyone who has ever written anything. I am no exception. I am merely an additional email address on a mailing list that expires as incessantly as the sun rises and sets. If they send out enough of these quick fixes for writer's block or some other malady that is impeding the writing of the great American novel (no, I don't have the stomach to write a novel), just a little bit of a return will repay them for their effort. Wonder what the expected return is on these mailings. In research, it's about 2–5%, and that's good.

So, the solicitations come in, and they go immediately into the trash can, or I mark them for my spam folder. Sorry, guys, but you have no magic for $75 or $39.95 or whatever the price is this week. You can watch videos, do tutorials, make lists and keep yourself convinced that that novel is coming out, but it's probably not. And, even if it does come out, now you have to accept yet another solicitation that will give you the golden recipe needed to get an agent, write a cover letter, and get published. You are on your way to a Hamptons retreat, my friend, and it's only $49.95 and you're there! Not so fast. Let me tell you a little story.

I was in a few particularly good spots in my career in media, and at one, the idea suddenly hit me that I wanted to do an interview piece with Woody Allen. I guess I'd seen one of his films, or I'd seen him on one of his appearances on late-night TV. Who knows where the idea came from, but I thought I just might be able to swing it because of where I was at the time. I'll leave that little tidbit out. It's really not necessary. If you've ever worked anywhere that has some juice with people in the entertainment industry, you know what I mean.

How do I go about this task and get myself a really good interview with this somewhat erratic comedian turned filmmaker? The first step, of course, was to find out who I had to speak to in order to get through to him. A series of brief discussions and a few phone calls later produced a name. This guy was the go-to man for any interviews, appearances or whatever with Woody Allen, and I, in all my chutzpah, called him.

Prior to trying to set up this appointment with Allen, I had managed to, can you believe this, get Penthouse magazine to agree that they would like an interview piece with him. So, now I had a magazine with pretty good circulation (at that time), and all I needed was the interview and my trusty tape recorder. It was going so smoothly that I thought it actually might happen.

I set out to find everything I could about him—where he lived, what he liked to do, where he had lunch (if there was a regular spot), how he saw himself as a filmmaker, etc. Some of the tidbits were quite interesting, but I decided they should be left out of any piece I might produce. Everyone needs a bit of privacy, and I wasn't about to be some type of investigative reporter here. It would be a straightforward piece on his vision and where he thought he'd go with it.

A few more phone calls were made, messages were left, and finally a brief discussion with the wunderkind who had access and the glitch came up. Sure he would consider interviewing with me, but there was one thing that he absolutely must have. What was that? He wanted to be on the cover of Penthouse. This is serious business. Or maybe it was that Penthouse wanted him to be on the cover with two nude women. The details began to get fuzzy, but that was it.

I waited for a week or more, and then I got the call that I didn't want. He wouldn't do it. No, he was not interested in being interviewed by anyone writing an article for Penthouse, no matter what they offered. There was no way the man could convince him. That was it.

How could he refuse that golden opportunity? Wouldn't it have been hilarious for him to be photographed for the cover with two or more gorgeous, scantily clad women? Nah, it wasn't what he wanted to do.

I'd go on to interview other writers and even a few actors backstage on Broadway. One visit was particularly interesting for the sudden appearance of a man in a sickly greenish suit carrying a physician's bag. The star needed a vitamin shot, and I was dispatched back to the street without an interview. But it was interesting just to climb down the rickety stairs after flashing my NYPD press pass, walk through the really shabby hallways beneath the theater, and finally come out into something like the production of a Boy Scout troupe. What these stars have to endure backstage most of their fans never know.

Woody, it was probably a good decision on your part. I would have loved it, but I totally understand why you nixed it. Now back to the film.

Chapter Thirty-Three

Chapter 33: A Year of Diaphoresis

Medical terms aren't meant to be mysterious. They're intended to quickly communicate to other medicos the current status of a patient, but anyone not in the healthcare field finds it so much gibberish. It's not for we uneducated to understand; we rationalize, and that's okay as long as they know what they're doing, but that's not always the case.

There are so many patients that I can recall at the many places I've worked that it's like reading a familiar book of short stories, only O'Henry didn't write these. These tales were lived and carefully nudged into whatever chemical structure comprises our memories, but they live, nevertheless, and so it is today. Occasionally, one boops to the surface like a swimmer asking to be noticed, and maybe that's what memory is: the reliving of moments not to be forgotten and jogged by some small thing in our present lives. I'll resist the temptation to become philosophical here.

The day started out like so many with morning meetings, patient groups, walks to other buildings for yet more meetings, chart reviews, informal hallway chats and admissions. The admissions one was where I first saw him from afar.

A young man, probably in his middle 20s or so, with long, oily hair in tangles, dirty, torn clothing and totally incoherent in his speech. It was not unusual except for one thing: he was diaphoretic, and that was a bit unusual. Patients admitted to psychiatric hospitals aren't usually in any medical distress, and it appeared this young man was—or was he? Not being an MD, I dismissed it as something to be evaluated by the physicians on the unit. No, it wasn't a mind-body thing and, therefore, not in my province of expertise.

The next day, I learned that he had been transferred from the Admissions unit (quite an an unusual quick transfer) to a unit for the severely disturbed, not the hospital unit. Again, somewhat of an unusual move for a patient who appeared to be in some type of medical distress. I happened to be on that unit that day and saw him seated in a chair where a muscular male nurse was carefully combing and cutting his hair. I never knew shampoo was such a good medium for cutting hair, but that's what the nurse was using.

He sat just staring ahead, and once in awhile he would blurt something out, but it was totally indistinguishable. No one knew what he was saying, but he was docile and allowed the cutting continue, so no restraints were required here. I did notice, however, that he was still diaphoretic, and the nurse remarked that they'd already changed his clothes twice that day because he was sweating so much. Why was he sweating? The ward physician had looked at him but didn't have him transferred to the hospital unit. Why? No answer. That was the way it was, and no one questioned it.

Weeks later, I inquired about the patient and was told that they couldn't figure out his diagnosis. He was still sweating profusely, had been pulling his teeth out, and no one could get through to him. Not violent, but seriously agitated. Can you think for just a moment how you'd feel if you were feeling awful, probably psychotic and couldn't get anyone to understand your needs? It must have been incredibly mentally painful.

The months went on, and I worked at other units at the vast hospital where I was transferred to the hospital unit at one point. It had been a year since that patient had been brought in, and I questioned one of the physicians. I was told that they just couldn't figure out the problem,, and he was still sweating as before. If I said I was shocked, that wouldn't even come close to my disbelief about the way this young man was being treated. Why hadn't he been transferred to an outside medical facility? No one seemed to know or cared to ask about it. Life went on, and they just did their jobs as before as though he never existed.

A few years later, I was talking to a colleague, and I mentioned this patient. I wondered what had happened to him. The colleague vaguely remembered him and said he'd died. They thought he might have had AIDS-related dementia. Yes, yes, I know what you must be thinking. How could this happen, and if it were AIDS, didn't anyone consider the contagion factor? Well, in a hospital where they didn't know sodium bicarbonate from sodium pentothal, it wasn't surprising. And where the psychiatric nurses didn't know what they were seeing with some patients was called akathisia and not "the Mellaril shuffle"; it shouldn't have surprised me.

I got out alive and healthy. The young man never made it.

Chapter Thirty-Four

Chapter 34: Just a Pen, Not a Payment

Medicine is a lot of things these days. It is a science and an art at the same time, but it's also a business and an opportunity. The latter two aspects of this profession, or, as one elderly physician I know says, it is a "calling," provide a dilemma for some and a bit of extra cash for others.

No doubt about it, ethics plays a big role here, and some of the major forces in medicine have tried to address the touchy problem of ethics. Limits have been placed on just how expensive those nifty little gifts to newly minted physicians can be and what can be accepted in good conscience. However, similar to any legal document, there is potential for interpretation. How do you interpret not accepting cash gifts but allowing "funds to be distributed to recipients without specific attribution to sponsors?" So, giving away some money but not saying who gave it? But doesn't that still mean it came from some sponsors of such programs, and doesn't that have a halo effect on every sponsor participating?

In prior years, I was bemused as the young medical students who were about to graduate whooped and hollered when they saw the shiny stethoscopes, the textbooks, the pens, the tablets, and even the software. It was like Christmas in late spring for them, and they delighted in it. Some, with rather grim countenances, announced that they were giving it all to the local healthcare clinic. They were in the minority of the group merriment. Others just delighted in all of it. So this was what medicine was about to give them. It was wonderful. Sure, that was years ago, and, sure, things have changed.

I have worked at several hospitals and healthcare settings over the years, and I've also sat in waiting rooms both as a patient and a member of a research team. The waiting room experiences are familiar to anyone who has watched the detail (aka salespersons) come and quickly be ushered into the office.

On some occasions, the person (used to be men; now it's shapely, well-dressed young women) would be carrying expensive textbooks or small pieces of computer equipment. On others, the salesperson was followed by one or two men carrying large trays of steaming food for a lunchtime presentation to the staff. Education, after all, is necessary in medicine, and staff training is essential. But it's also nice to have someone pay for your lunch as you sit quietly and watch them run through their slide presentations.

Some jobs I've had allowed me to see physicians sneaking out (yes, sneaking out) of the office to give presentations of prepared slides to physicians and other healthcare workers. Last time I questioned one, he got $1,500 for each of his efforts—all while he was receiving his salary as a full-time employee at an agency. I only know because I had to help him figure out how to use a USB drive on a computer. But is he any different from the psychiatrist who held five full-time jobs (all at the same time) at various facilities? Or the other psychiatrist who signed in at one job, went to another full-time job, and then, at the end of the day, went to the other to sign out? Of course, he's retired now and left instructions that he was to have no forwarding address provided to anyone.

Now a physician who has also seen the underbelly in its unattractive presentation has provided another look at medicine from his perspective. You can read it in "*Doctored: The Disillusionment of an American Physician*" if you wish. In it, according to reviewers, is an often unpalatable view of profiteering, cronyism, unnecessary testing and generally reprehensible behavior on the part of those who have sworn to do no harm.

Again, there's that tricky little wordplay. Doing "no harm" to whom or what? Do they harm the patient or society as a whole when they order unnecessary, very expensive testing that the rest of us will pay for? How about "no harm" if a patient is exposed time and time again to potentially harmful x-rays or other radiation? Well, I'll let one reviewer from the Yale School of Medicine respond when they wrote that the book is "a fantastic tour through the seedy underworld of American medicine." Enough said on that account.

A physician I respect once told me that he had breakfast each morning on a regular basis with peers at a major hospital. One of the peers is an orthopedic surgeon who, when he was leaving the table, would regularly joke, "Well, got to be off to do another unnecessary surgery." He was joking, surely. Is there a common joke in medicine about surgeons? *Go to a surgeon, and you get surgery*. Do they imply that you get it whether you need it or not? Oh, no, it can't be true.

What's the remedy for all of this? Tighter control by someone or some agency? It doesn't always work because of the lobbying that's involved, and we consumers have no lobbyists to speak of. Should hospitals ride roughshod on fast-and-loose physicians? Not when they're the ones who bring in all the money and fund all those extensive building projects. Will the new trend of hiring physicians away from private practice and making them hospital employees help? Do you think so?

All it comes down to is caveat emptor, as it does when you buy anything. You're buying or paying for a service, and you have a right to negotiate, get a second opinion, or begin a grassroots movement against anything you see needs fixing. Yes, it's left on your already burdened shoulders.

Chapter 35: Remembering a Fork

Celebrity chefs such as Wolfgang Puck, we read, are now offering a gourmet touch to services such as Meals on Wheels, and even the Culinary Institute of America is offering classes aimed at the nursing home crowd. The burgeoning of the elderly and the old-old residents requiring nursing home care or assisted living is growing rapidly. This provides a tidy incentive to those corporations serving them.

All well and good, you say, because why shouldn't this group of seniors enjoy the pleasures of fine dining? I agree, but I wonder, too, about the cost of the establishments that are offering this fare. Not everyone has the means to move to a premier senior residential facility or nursing home. What kind of foods do they receive, and who prepares them? The bottom line everywhere is, of course, cost and that will always be the prime motivator. I once visited an upscale nursing home that offered a glass of wine with Sunday dinner, and physicians even ordered one cocktail per day for specific residents. The nurses station kept the booze in a locked cabinet ready for the evening dispensing.

The "chef," aka the cook, at this facility where families pay close to $100K/year or more for a family member, was a woman who was intellectually challenged. She did her best and cooked what she knew, but it was always the same meals with little taste. Of course, it was explained to me that the residents didn't like their food seasoned, and it was left to them. But how could they season anything when seasoning is an integral part of food preparation and salt and pepper just don't cut it?

As I read this article regarding the increasing turn to fresh, locally grown vegetables and more exotic foods, I also wondered not only about those who can't afford it but also those who don't recognize it. It took me back to a time a few decades ago when I saw what up-close and personal reveals to you about dementia and Alzheimer's. I should mention that one of the chefs is even taking chicken and pureeing it in a blender, then remolding it to look like a chicken and garnishing it with a reduction of some type. Good stuff, you'd agree, I'm sure. But what if you won't recognize it as food? What if the sight of a "chicken" on your plate frightens you?

Alzheimer's takes away more than just memory; it robs you of the ability to independently make simple decisions like eating. I watched as a woman in a hospital sat staring at her plate. There was no movement, and she was urged to eat. The problem was that she didn't know what she was expected to do, and she didn't know what the utensils were for. Eating had turned into a trial, and anything in front of her, including the utensils, was for eating. In fact, she did pick up a fork and try to eat it. How did they permit it to get to this discouraging point?

One of the amusing aspects of nursing home life, if you can find this amusing, is that the dining room becomes much like a high school cafeteria. There are seats for the assorted cliques, and if you attempt to join that table, you are quickly and sometimes sharply told to go elsewhere. Yes, dementia does affect those really important frontal lobes involved in decision-making and adhering to social rules.

Staff must be quite diligent in helping new residents to their tables and ensuring that they will fit in well with the other established members of that table. The plan is to mix some good talkers in with those who can use verbal stimulation. No one actually measures how well this plan works. Does it encourage or discourage talking or bring up other issues? Interesting things to explore.

Meals may be changing, and there may be a lot of media aimed at this effort, but how the residents are helped is equally important. Not all of them are so sanguine about the current changes

Chapter 36: One Day to Remember

There is one question that will always elicit an historic response when asked and it is, "Where were you when..." The "when," of course, can stand for many of us to be September 11, 2001, or November 22, 1963 and the memory, forever frozen in our memories as though it were yesterday, is easily retrieved and recounted. So, where were you on that fateful day? Were you in Manhattan or New York, the United States, Europe or the West Coast? Where were you and what did you think had happened?

Many September 11s have come and today the most recent is almost gone, but we will never forget. Yesterday, passing by a modest home in a local neighborhood, I noticed a lone, handmade sign stretched across the lawn that read simply, "September 11, 2001, we will never forget."

I didn't ask anyone where they were today and, frankly, I almost forgot and that sounds so contrary to what that simple sign said.

Today, I did forget and I wonder why I did. I wasn't particularly busy; I had plenty of time to review any of the articles in the media, on the Internet, on TV or short reports on the radio. Perhaps I needed to forget even though I wasn't in Manhattan on that horrific day. Perhaps I was exhibiting a mental weariness of all the war coverage blasting our way over so many years now. Perhaps I had become numbed by it all. But I know there are others who will not have such an easy time on this day. They were in the buildings, and they bear a burden that will never disappear and, for some, never be lightened by the years to come.

I was across the Hudson River in New Jersey, sitting in a cramped, windowless office surrounded by physicians working away reviewing disability reports. I was reviewing the reports on my desk when the phone rang. A friend told me something I thought was a poor joke or a scenario from one of the disaster films showing then. She said that a plane had hit one of the towers of the World Trade Center, and I blurted that out to the entire office. Heads jerked up, and one physician searched a desk drawer for a tiny transistor radio that had just one station on it, a news station.

As we listened to the news, we surmised it was a plane that had gone out of control, like the one that had hit the Empire State Building decades ago. Then, she reported that another plane had hit a tower, and one word came out of a physician's mouth, "It's an attack. It's terrorists." Stunned, we sat not knowing what to do. My friend urged me to leave and go home. It was just around 9AM on a bright, beautiful morning, the same kind of morning it had been in Dallas on November 22, 1963.

All of us looked blankly at each other, and I announced that I was leaving. The trip down the elevator and over to the garage was one of the strangest I've ever experienced. Strangers talked to each other on the street about the attack and wished each other a safe trip home.

One portion of my trip took me to a point on a turnpike that was perpendicular to lower Manhattan, where I saw the enormous brownish-grey cloud engulfing lower Manhattan and drifting lazily north on the edge of the Hudson. The turnpike, too, had an eerie feel about it with dump trucks closing off exits and screeching fire trucks and ambulances racing south toward the tunnel. Cars drove over grass to get off at exits closed, and everything was incredibly quiet with the exception of the sirens.

The rest of the day isn't so sharply defined, but I do know I called at least one person I knew who worked in one of the towers and left a voice message expressing my concern for her safety. I would learn a week later that she had made it out, but there had been perilously close brushes with death and sights no one should ever see in their lifetime.

So, today is another day of remembrance and tears and a determination to make something good from this very bad, bad thing. Why do I still think of it, sometimes, as reminiscent of "*The Bridge of San Luis Rey*?" I guess it's the intertwining of stories and lives then and afterward. Occasionally, I hear of another odd twist of fate related to that tragedy, and each time there's one of those OMG moments.

What can you say about all of this? New Yorkers and Americans showed a resilience they may not have known they had. There was a cohesiveness during the days that followed that offered some comfort, and, in fact, we did comfort each other as I'd never seen before.

I may have thought I forgot it today, but I didn't. There would always be something to bring that horror back, even if it was the opening of a museum or capping the new tower. The souls still linger, and they will not be forgotten.

Chapter
Thirty-Seven

Chapter 37: Not Just Another Day in May 1970

American history is rich with tales untold and those too-often told, but in a manner that is sometimes either unfaithful to the events or a sickening attempt to fatten the bottom line. Which was it when Urban Outfitters offered a replica of a blood-stained Kent State sweatshirt for sale at $130, a garment that was being offered on ebay for $550? Is this a reminder of our recent, bloody past or someone's worse-than-crass attempt at "humor" in the service of corporate profit? Two words suffice: disgusting and shameful.

Perhaps the designer was so poorly educated that he/she didn't fully appreciate what happened that May day in 1970 when four college students, exercising their right to assemble and protest, were gunned down by the local National Guard unit. Bleeding and dying on the college quad, one became the subject of an iconic photo that stands today as a symbol of presidential anarchy.

The president in question, one Richard M. Nixon, a man who was almost disbarred for attempting to influence a juror when he was first admitted to the bar, deemed the students dirty hippies. Did hippies attend college? I thought they had "turned on, tuned in and dropped out" as Timothy Leary suggested was the appropriate reaction to political fascism in the form of Nixon.

I suppose you could say it was a "tribute" of sorts to those dead students, but I can't buy that. It was in a distorted attempt at innovative design if you were not totally in touch with reality, I suppose. Similar to the recent shirt offered by yet another hip and edgy designer. The shirt, for those who missed it, was similar to the uniforms worn by the captives in the concentration camps in Europe during World War II. Oh, so trendy and creative, why would anyone protest? Lord knows, except for the fact that more than six million people died while wearing those garments.

Gee, why not put out a Matthew Shepard t-shirt with, perhaps, a really gory, realistic portrayal of him being crucified on that Wyoming fence? Wouldn't that be too cool for words? Oh, yeah, they could sell it everywhere. Quick, what color scheme should we pick?

Or maybe a Harvey Milk shirt riddled with bullet holes? We could make a really nice jig with nails to simulate the bullets. Or was he shot in the head? If he were shot in the head, it would ruin the whole design. Must look that one up on Google. Thank God for Google; it lets us keep all that history stuff available, and we don't have to open even one book. Don't you love it?

Perhaps a clothing line called "Strange Fruit" with lots of really wonderful portrayals of African-American men hanging from trees?

Wow, that would be great. You could position a few of them on one tree sort of like Christmas ornaments. Don't you just love it?

Maybe we might even go a bit more retro and dream up something with a civil rights theme? There's that wonderful trio (or was it four?) of little girls in the Birmingham church explosion, Mrs. Violet Liuzzo, who was helping the Freedom Riders, or even Chaney, Goodman and Schwerner. So much to choose from during that era that you really have a hard time choosing.

Ask yourself who was sitting on their brains the day they decided that a Kent State sweatshirt was a good idea? How many people with an absence of good sense and decency were in the room when the mock-ups were passed around? Did not one voice speak out in protest?

The shirt is no longer being offered, but oh, how the melody lingers on for Urban Outfitters. How will you redeem yourselves, guys?

Chapter Thirty-Eight

Chapter 38: I Was Hallucinating

The vocabulary of children and pre-teens is limited by both their experience and their schooling. Granted, some kids have a more robust grasp of the language, but it is usually limited in certain areas. One of those areas is in the psychiatric sphere as well as in matters related to sexual abuse. The latter has been well-documented in the professional literature, which discusses how to adequately and appropriately ferret out information from children regarding possible abuse.

Some clinicians, inadequately trained but hopefully with the best of intentions, have caused incredible harm to the kids, their families and those who have been accused of abuse. We don't need to go further than the infamous McMartin Daycare trial to see evidence of what happens when the inexperienced are called to interview children on sex abuse. But sex abuse isn't the only crime against children. Another, unnoticed and just as harmful, one is perpetrated when poorly trained mental health professionals (psychiatrists, too) interview children.

Do a simple Google search on *False Memory Syndrome* and who supports it, and you will enter a world that is surreal in its non-reality. And no one needs to look very far to find this type of problem in their own communities. Claims of abuse seem to be rife in all too many divorce actions, and you have to wonder what would be the reason to mount such an attack against someone. One psychologist on the East Coast recently had her license pulled for *her lack of training regarding children's sexual abuse* despite her claims of being an expert witness in divorce cases.

Cases of what results when a psychiatrist or other mental health professional interviews children relative to specific behaviors are too many to document here. The result is often life-long stigma and the administration of powerful, unnecessary medications. These kids carry an invisible mark on their foreheads (metaphorically speaking, of course), much like the infamous Scarlet Letter, that cannot be erased, and life will not be easy for these kids. How many kids now carry this designation? I suggest you read whatever Dr. Allen Francis has written in his blogs or books about psychiatric medication and diagnosis of kids with ADHD. But it doesn't stop there, apparently.

Sometimes evidence comes unexpectedly in the form of a comment by a child, and when it does, you need to stop and question yourself regarding how it came to be. Here's just one example. A young boy, having a wonderful time at a family celebration, became overheated from too vigorous dancing. Relatives quickly responded to his condition, which was apparent from his red, sweating head and somewhat unsteady gait. He was overheated and needed to be taken aside to cool down and rest and that was being done when he unexpectedly said, "I was hallucinating."

Hallucinating? What child knows that term? It's not in the books they read. It's not in the video games they play or the music they listen to, so how did it suddenly enter his vocabulary? Well, a psychiatrist who had performed a school exam (of course, to see if he had ADHD) asked if he had ever heard voices that weren't there or seen things that weren't there.

Let me be clear here. In my over 30 years in the field, seeing things that don't exist usually is a sign of a few things, such as drug use, nervous system infection, brain tumor, medication side effects or malingering ("I see shadows" is a famous one here). Even persons with schizophrenia don't usually "see things." I'm not saying it doesn't happen, but it's not as usual as you might think, except in the mind of a poorly trained or sometimes disinterested clinician. Patients in hospitals often interpret this reference to "voices" to mean their own thoughts and not actual voices. But when they do misunderstand and report it, it goes down as an auditory hallucination or AH.

The boy's interview with the psychiatrist was just such an instance of childhood misunderstanding and negligence on the part of the psychiatrist to delve further. If he had, the boy would have told him, as he later told his mother, that the "voices" he hears are what his mother has told him to do or not to do at home or in school. It wasn't a hallucination at all; it was a memory of what was expected in the home and in school. But the doc put it down as an AH, and, of course, they would have to consider antipsychotic medication (AP for those non-clinicians here) and consider it soon. After all, this child might be dangerous. Think someone is dangerous, and you may very well bring on the very behavior you are afraid of. Actions do speak louder than words. Teachers, please take special note here.

Careful interviewing of children is not something that should be taken lightly. Specialized training and in-person continuing education should be mandatory yearly before anyone attempts this delicate task. The life that is saved may be that of the child, and, certainly, misery for the family can be avoided as well as huge outlays for unnecessary and damaging medications.

Why has the use of AP and ADHD medications spiked so dramatically over the prior decade? See what Dr. Francis has to say about it. I'll leave it to him to more fully flesh this one out for you should you be seeking a highly qualified expert on this matter.

Let's not label kids for life without erring on the side of caution first. More conservative approaches are far better than rushing to preparations that immediately rush to the emerging brain and which may do damage that cannot be undone.

Chapter 39: A Reflex to Damage

Sports and all the training and repeated drills aimed at honing an individual's skills all depend on one thing: a reflex. No, this isn't the reflex you expect to see in a physician's office where they tap your knee or elbow with a rubber hammer. These reflexes are more dependent on your immediate, instinctual reactions that are almost unconscious. There are certain sports, however, where the reflex can become an impediment when not engaged in this actual physical and mental combat aimed at winning.

The success or failure in a sport is highly dependent on these reflexes. Some are intended to defend against a blow, others to quickly respond to a volley on a tennis court. Likewise, some sports are intended not only to develop a sense of self-confidence and personal mastery over emotional impulses but also a respect for others. There is no need in sports such as karate or aikido to be seen as more than the master of the execution of the moves as well as the master of one's self.

Asian martial arts are a personal physical and emotional journey of control over emotion with the knowledge that you could easily inflict a formidable injury, if not death, on any opponent. Killing, especially in karate, is ridiculously easy. This understanding of the danger in one's hands and feet is not to be taken lightly and must be ever under control. It's the same with prizefighters whose hands are considered lethal weapons.

Endless hours are spent learning this control, and the masters constantly reinforce skill with restraint. The same is true in many other sports, of course, but in too many sports there is an emphasis on massive attacks on the opponent of the moment. The reflex is to injure, to stop at all costs, and to ensure the opponent will not be able to continue. Muscle is behind much of this effort as well as a credo to "rip their heads off" as I've heard high school coaches urge their football teams to do. It isn't a sport; it's a clash to demolish the opponent.

If you are constantly training to "rip their heads off" or you're paid a bonus for causing major physical damage to the other team, how do you put that philosophy into your pocket when you leave the field? The reflex you've been taught is always there, but you haven't received any of that special training found in the Asian martial arts, and that's where a major void exists.

Overriding all of this training is years of being pampered and "handled" when interpersonal problems arise off the field. There was always someone there to make sure you didn't fumble because you were a warhorse churning out billions of dollars every year for your owners. Yes, you have owners even though you think of yourself as having a contract. Lose the contract and you lose your livelihood, something you worked for your entire life. It isn't going to be pretty, but this sense of entitlement and the reflex were both there working against the sports workers.

New term, yes, but aren't they "workers," and aren't they chained to contracts that can be terminated for infractions (aka loopout for cancellation) or failure to produce? They are surely workers just as anyone in an office is a worker. Call them athletes, if you must, but it's just another name for them. Yes, I dismiss all those years of toil to perfect their athletic skills, I know. Pare the skills away, if you can for a moment, and you have a worker. Just that simple, and without a job, what is a worker, especially one with no other skills than the one he used in the job he just lost? Unemployed.

The recent spate of domestic violence incidents among football players and even a judge in the South have, as the media is hammering home, opened a window into the private pain caused by this sense of privilege and reckless reflexes to damage. Perhaps there is good from bad again in the form of social media outcries to begin to take more stringent actions against the offenders and to help the objects of their viciousness.

The primary question now is whether there is true conviction or convenient public relations actions to quell the outcries. The game has changed, but we can expect that it may not change that much. Everyone has rights, and the athletes or others who fail to act in a civilized manner will sue whenever any action is taken against them. Major advertisers are already standing back, waiting to see just how strong and effective these new social media forces are or if they will die out given enough time and some tepid corrective actions.

The NFL had a mandatory course in domestic violence for new team members when Ray Rice joined the team. Now, it must be questioned as to the effectiveness of this program and how successful the new programs that are being formulated will be. It's not just domestic violence or violence toward others; a major change in personality seems to be needed. But how could any employer do this? Seems highly improbable, especially when the star athletes will still be pampered and protected for the good of the team and the corporate sponsors.

So where do they begin in order to address this particular psychological infection? It begins where everything begins, in childhood, but there's no going back for those adults who have lashed out in violence. They will have to look deeply into themselves and see who they are, if they can, and then take any actions they can to redress these egregious actions against women and children.

And let's help them with a beginning question for their inward look: What man beats a child to the point that he has a gash on his head and/or legs and includes his scrotum in the lashing? And, for good measure, what type of man knocks a woman out and then drags her out of an elevator? Was she a match for him? Cheap shot in the extreme.

Chapter 40: Domestic Abuse Is an "Equal Opportunity" Offense

An uncomfortable bright light has been shining on domestic violence and sports figures during the past several weeks, but that is only the tip of this abuse iceberg. The abuse receiving media attention has centered on heterosexual couples and failed to note the abuse prevalence in same-sex relations. Here, however, it may be even worse than we thought, and it isn't something that sprung anew with marriage equality.

One study suggested that same-sex domestic violence is even more prevalent than it is in heterosexual relationships. Abusers are everywhere, and the patterns are startlingly similar. The one difference here is that societal mores, fear of ostracism or other consequences keep victims from reporting the violence. Whether they are gay, homosexual, lesbian or LGBT, not everyone is "out" as the media might have us believe, and this keeps them victimized.

One prime, yet formerly secretive, domestic abuse situation occurred back in the 1980s to Olympic diving champ Greg Louganis. He discussed the relationship and how it affected him in his book, *Breaking the Surface*. One incident, with a knife to his throat, was not only frightening; it also involved rape. Reading this, someone might be questioning how a man who was an Olympic champion, handsome and muscular could be so traumatized by another man that he failed to defend himself. But that's just the point because abusers pick their victims carefully and seek out their areas of vulnerability and then exploit that knowledge to remain in power.

But first, of course, they take a few note pages from the pedophile's playbook where it suggests the abuse begins by preparing the victim. This includes being overly attentive, generous, loving and kind. This deflects any internal mental defensive shields and lays the groundwork of vulnerability. It is as carefully crafted as a spider weaving a web to entangle its prey.

The web is woven, all elements of danger are removed, and then the spider springs into action. Aside from physical assaults, there are the many reinforcing psychological assaults on self-perception, worthlessness, potential financial dependence and guilt for bringing on the violence. The victim now begins to victimize themselves, a role the perpetrator works hard at reinforcing.

Some of the aspects of same-sex domestic abuse that are different from heterosexual couple abuse have been outlined by services offering information. One service notes the following:

"Gay or lesbian batterers will threaten 'outing" their victims to work colleagues, family, and friends. This threat is amplified by the sense of extreme isolation among gay and lesbian victims since some are still closeted from friends and family, have fewer civil rights protections, and lack access to the legal system.

Lesbian and gay victims are more reluctant to report abuse to legal authorities. Survivors may not contact law enforcement agencies because doing so would force them to reveal their sexual orientation or gender identity.

Gay and lesbian victims are also reluctant to seek help out of fear of showing a lack of solidarity among the gay and lesbian community. Similarly, many gay men and women hide their abuse out of a heightened fear that society will perceive same-sex relationships as inherently dysfunctional.

Gay and lesbian victims are more likely to fight back than are heterosexual women. This can lead law enforcement to conclude that the fighting was mutual, overlooking the larger context of domestic violence and the history of power and control in the relationship.

Abusers can threaten to take away the children from the victim. In some states, adoption laws do not allow same-sex parents to adopt each other's children. This can leave the victim with no legal rights should the couple separate. The abuser can easily use the children as leverage to prevent the victim from leaving or seeking help. Even when the victim is the legally recognized parent, an abuser may threaten to out the victim to social workers hostile to gays and lesbians, which may result in a loss of custody. In the worst cases, the children can even end up in the custody of the abuser."

The abuser, therefore, uses social stigma and the fear of a lack of acceptance and help as potent weapons against the victim. In one study of gay individuals in Venezuela, there was a fear of reporting abuse to the police since the police were feared. The media has covered a sufficient number of accounts of individuals who were sworn to protect the citizenry and who nevertheless used force and fear against those same individuals. The number of incidents of street violence against gay persons, too, magnifies the fear of being outed and placed at greater risk for personal safety or even maintaining their livelihood.

Our culture is not as gay-friendly as we would like to believe, and while those in certain positions of power or with extraordinary wealth may proclaim their sexuality for all to hear, they are outliers, it would seem. Not everyone can or is willing to take the chance of being further victimized. Research studies, therefore, pale when it comes to actually revealing the true extent of this particular area of domestic violence.

Anyone wishing for more information may contact the **GLBT National Help Center**, where services on a variety of topics are available to the community or families in need of assistance.

Chapter 41: Pedophiles Are the Nicest People

Take a moment to ask yourself a question. Do you know anyone who is a pedophile or a child pornographer? Give it some thought. Chances are, you may, but you'd never know it just as the parents of six 10–11-year-old girls in a science class in an elementary school didn't know about their teacher. Highly thought of, respected, and attentive to the students, you name it, this fellow had it in aces, but it was all in the service of his predilection for sexually abusing young girls. We don't know if he also went after boys, but that's not the concern here. The concern is that pedophiles move among us easily and without a hint of suspicion. They are, in fact, those who are above suspicion.

The parents of a particular pediatrician in New Jersey never suspected that their wonderful, sensitive and oh-so-kid-friendly doc was also a pedophile until one mother filed a complaint after her daughter related an unpleasant touching incident in the exam room while she wasn't present. Later, his office computer was found to have thousands of child pornography photos on it and, of course, he said he was "doing research," just as I've heard other pedophiles use that explanation.

Of course, when your primary job is the supervision of young boys delivering the local newspaper, you have to wonder how qualified the guy I spoke to was in researching child pornography. In his home, however, he had at least three packed file cabinets with child pornography, and then people began to question those overnight camping trips for the boys and the swimming lessons that involved diving off his shoulders.

Another case, where two young boys came forward to a relative about the fear and discomfort they had about their mother's boyfriend, was ultimately dismissed by the authorities. The reason? Simple. The kids had ADHD, and their stories couldn't possibly be believed even though they had, in private sessions, told more than one social worker and a child psychologist what had happened to each of them. The boys, by the way, never told each other what had happened to them. They were too ashamed and frightened that even worse things would happen to them.

The kids, for the time being, are living with a relative, but there is a remote possibility that they may be returned to the abuser's household. How do you handle that scenario without causing the children to "act out" as the school authorities like to say? But the courts, in their sometimes misguided wish to reunite families, do send children back into these familial torture chambers where they are physically abused and raped by men who have cleverly selected women with small children. Too many times, the children end up dead, and the family is united at a funeral.

Do you know where one of the best places to find these vulnerable women might be for a pedophile on the hunt? Why, of course, it's Parents Without Partners. That is not to say that the groups don't actively try to protect group members from becoming prey for these monsters in sheep's clothing. But the true intent is so cleverly concealed that even these groups can be hoodwinked into providing entree to women with child victims. They also provide an unbelievable opportunity to rape vulnerable, single moms and they threaten to harm the children if the woman doesn't comply.

The American Academy of Child & Adolescent Psychiatry estimates that there are 80K reported instances of child sexual abuse each year, but this is far below the actual number. The reasons these crimes against children are not reported may be because the child fears the perpetrator, they have been warned that their siblings or parents will be harmed, the child is ashamed and is told they are to blame for the abuse, they fear retaliation by their parents or loss of love, and they are told no one will believe them.

Of course, there are too many instances of persons in the ministry who sexually abuse children, and they, for years, were protected by their orders, and no reports were made to the police. The trauma that ensues can result in many types of behavioral changes as well as depression and suicide. How should a person respond to any report of child sexual abuse? The Academy offers guidelines on their website.

Of one thing we can be sure: children are vulnerable. Trust is a wonderful thing, but children need to be helped to understand that not every adult is to be obeyed or to be trusted. That is not to say that children should be so frightened and intimidated that they respond with fear to everyone. It is not an easy task, but parents, guardians and persons in positions of authority need to help train children to be aware that they have rights and there are actions to be taken when someone does something that makes them uncomfortable.

When I was involved with one national organization, we talked to parents about "Good Touch, Bad Touch" and the need for a secret word to be used in emergency situations. The word was used whenever a stranger said a parent wanted them to go with them. "What's the secret word?" the child would ask. Then the child would immediately leave to seek safety in a neighbor's home, a store or a school.

Another was to train children to counter the popular ploy of a stranger asking a child to help them find their puppy. Kids don't immediately think about the peculiarity of an adult asking a child for help in finding a lost dog. Their response must not be a knee-jerk one of agreeing to help, and it takes training to ingrain this skill in the children's repertoire of responses. Just as you teach a child to read or to know their numbers, you need to teach them to act in a situation of doubt.

Today, an ex-archbishop was arrested by the Vatican for sex crimes against children, and a science teacher in a New York City school was also arrested. Tomorrow it could be a police officer, a physician or a trusted neighbor, friend, coach, tutor or even a relative. Predators are everywhere, and they don't have easily distinguished signs that you can detect.

The moral is to let children know that they need to learn certain basic rules or actions for self-protection and for you to practice with them. Answer their questions with age-appropriate responses and always offer support and understanding.

Chapter Forty-Two

Chapter 42: The Wonder of the Internet

Using your computer can be a wonderful activity, pushing you to even greater productivity and exploration and helping solve issues that have come up in your work and personal life. Aren't you always hearing, "There's an app for that"?

It is an incredible contraption that, from a dumb combination of "0" and "1," turns inexplicably into hard work made simple. Computer coding, in fact, is for many absurdly simple yet elegant and sophisticated in what it does and at the incredible speed it completes these tasks.

Toss your fear aside, and when you've got some time, dip your toe into this incredible knowledge pool by picking up a copy of "Learn Python the Hard Way" (3rd edition) by Zed A. Shaw. I don't usually tout any books, but when it comes to learning Python, the language on which everything is being based (ok, maybe not everything), this is the book.

Not only is the paperback wonderful, it comes with a great DVD, and all the problem sets are in video format on YouTube. So, after you've tried your best and you get stuck, or maybe not, you can watch any of the 57 videos they've graciously provided and see where you may have had a little blip in your code. Everything is at your own pace, and you will master this programming code. Be confident.

Without making this blog entirely about one of the best, simplest computer coding programs around, let me use this example to explore another issue: when something goes wrong. It may be with your computer, your work situation, your financial situation or a myriad of other areas of your life. Many of these things will result in moments, if not more, of sheer panic. That can be paralyzing and often brings on that awful sweat that is the ugly companion of heightened anxiety. I know you've felt it, and you're not alone.

Step One to anything: Calm down; don't immediately rush to do something unless you have no choice. The "no choice" actions would fall into that "if I don't stop this fire now, it will burn down the house" category.

Step Two: Carefully assess that it's not a "burn down the house" situation and you do need a solution, but you also have the luxury of giving it some thought and time, even perhaps calling someone(s) in to consult with you. Remember the Exxon Valdez? I think they gave it a little thought before they ran off to rescue all those sea animals and tried to clean up the mess. But your situation may not be nearly as dire as that one.

Step Three: Always remember to start with the simple solutions. Why do you suppose all those computer geeks you call on the computer hotlines ask you to go through that fairly brainless series of steps involving shutting everything off, disconnection and reconnecting the plugs, etc.? Simple is always best and I am a great believer in this conservative approach.

You may not have to throw something out (could be software, your computer, your car, a business plan or whatever) because there may be a really simple solution that you haven't thought of or someone has decided not to tell you about. The latter involves people who get paid to solve your problems, and, sorry to say, auto mechanics do not have the best reputations, and some healthcare professionals seem to be in a hot race to gain that standing.

Step Four: Write down a detailed account of what you did, why, when and what the result was (once you solve it). This is your "go-to" file for the future. And remember that whatever you did in the past to solve a problem like this doesn't have to be replicated verbatim. You can modify it as needed because it may be a good bare-bones template starting point for something in the future. Never throw out your good work. Just keep it for future reference and consider it from many angles. Good work is good work.

The mantra for the future is: **Simple is best,** and that's where I begin.

Chapter 43: Those Who Are Forgotten

The recent high school shootings in Washington by a young man from a Native American family pulled up memories for me of a slight association with education and Native American reservations. It all happened because I taught a doctoral-level psychology course, and in it I had a student who was studying environmental issues. As part of his degree requirements, he had to spend one summer teaching on a reservation in the western part of the US. He was excited, as new teachers often are, to have this assignment. The excitement would soon cool when anticipation was smacked in the face by harsh reality.

It didn't take long for him to realize that not only was he faced with a total lack of teaching materials, but there was no library, almost no textbooks, no science materials and a tribal council that viewed him askance as an outsider. Cooperation would be like pulling teeth, and the kids weren't even in the middle. The kids seemed to be absolutely out of the equation. Pride, no small impediment in any procedure, was at stake and everything had to be done with the utmost attention to it.

There was no paucity of historic clashes and betrayals on the part of the US government, most probably the Bureau of Indian Affairs. The agency has as its mission "to enhance the quality of life, to promote economic opportunity, and to carry out the responsibility to protect and improve the trust assets of American Indians, Indian tribes and Alaska Natives."

Somehow, that mission statement drips with misguided paternalism and empty promises. It wouldn't take long for you to research the missteps of the BIA, especially as it pertains to education and economic opportunity. Be my guest and do a bit of hunting on this issue. Perhaps you will find things that could have been addressed, should have been addressed, or went completely awry in terms of this "mission." I believe that "assets of American Indians" includes the children who are born in these restrictive environments and then thrown into a school culture that is alien from their own.

How does the BIA not ensure that "economic opportunity" is provided initially in the form of libraries, books, science materials and qualified teachers if they are going to maintain schools on these reservations? Or do they not provide these schools any longer? What is the current role of the tribal councils? How can anyone trust, and how can it be gradually established? First, I think we should stop treating Native Americans like foreigners.

Aside from how we fail our Native Peoples, how are we not making use of an incredible talent pool for all kids in this country? Long-established groups of retired executives exist all across this country, and they readily offer free services to local businesses in need of the experience and talents of these individuals. Yet, we fail to form cohesive groups of talented individuals who could act as a senior mentor corps for kids in need. I'm not talking about just retired teachers, although they could be wonderful.

What I'm thinking about are engineers, computer programmers, biologists, environmentalists, etc. Kids need exposure to all that talent, and it's lying dormant and unused. What a terrible waste. Incredible value is unseen or unused. Is it because of politics? Or perhaps a lack of corporate realization that future employees will come from the ranks of today's school kids? Smart self-interest would seem prudent here, just as Xerox 40 years ago devised a plan to give up to a year off with pay for employees who came up with a plan for working with school kids.

Creativity is the buzzword these days, and entrepreneurship is praised and prized, but where is it in this instance? Completely lacking from my viewpoint. Prove me wrong. I think that would be a good thing.

Chapter 44: Ah, Those Terribly Simplistic Coaches

Not licensed, not regulated, without a code of ethics, and questionable training, life coaches are filling their bank accounts, but at whose expense?

Coach is a word that was once the exclusive province of those involved in some type of sports activity. Now, it has assumed the multi-purpose, all-encompassing aura of that other poorly used word, "clinic"/"clinical." I don't know about you, but I question the wisdom of both, and today's news in my email just solidified my concern as yet another guru poked his head forth as a newly minted "coach" for executive managers or would-be managers.

It reminded me of a very unpleasant experience I had many years ago while attending mandatory training at a psychiatric hospital. Staff were going to learn to be team players and to assert themselves on units that included quite possibly dangerous patients, including those who had murdered one or more people.

How were these coaches going to help us perform this magic? Oh, it was very simple, and that simplistic approach is still kicking around, but this time it's not free training but something that costs a big chunk of money.

Seated in a large auditorium-like room in the main building of the hospital were all newly hired staff, including psychiatrists, nurses, aides and psychologists. The interns didn't know how fortunate they were that their hospital stints didn't begin until after this lovely experience had concluded.

Two nurses, who had been trained by staff at a special facility, stood in front of us and informed us that we would begin each session (of which there would be one a day for five days) with our standing up and shouting as loud as we could, "Good caring!" We would do this several times as the nurses insisted we were not doing it loud enough, and they tried to whip up our enthusiasm.

So, everyone dutifully inhaled deeply and shouted to the rafters, "GOOD CARING!" Once they were satisfied, we were told to sit down again as they went over something akin to a speed course in neurobiology (the dumbest thing I've ever heard anywhere). A former housekeeping supervisor had devised the program and sold it to the institutions. His credentials? Nil, but that didn't deter management from buying his wares. He must have been an exceptional salesman.

I have serious doubts that any of this "good caring" really translated into anything but lost time away from our assigned duties. Certainly, it didn't enter into treatment plans, group therapy or even chart reviews from my perspective. The psychiatrists went right on going to sleep at team meetings, the nursing supervisors kept on writing nice little progress notes for patients they didn't know, and the staff continued as though "good caring" were a foreign land they had never visited. Money not well spent and time wasted, but we HAD been trained, and that looked good on the annual reports.

Shouting out something may make you feel good at the moment, although that's debatable, but does it provide any long-term results of import? I have to go back to the original thinking of Leon Festinger regarding actions and our belief systems.

Simply put, Festinger theorized that if your actions do not mesh well with your beliefs, you change your beliefs. What he didn't believe initially, in my experience, was that your actions don't always change your beliefs, as they hadn't at that hospital with that staff. Their actions were empty, and their belief systems were apparently unchanged as they plodded along in search of that next paycheck.

All good little boys and girls attended the sessions and obediently complied no matter how foolish they felt or how much they didn't believe this was useful. It was time away from work, and that was very good. After all, they were getting paid for this training, weren't they? And they could put it on their mandatory training sheets. How good was that? Paid for just sitting and shouting? And for five days in a row so that you could miss the morning meeting? Ah, heaven.

The quality of coaching or coaches cannot be judged by their name or what they promise or how much it costs. Results are what count, and you have to ask who is doing the counting and with what measures. You can't give out an evaluation sheet at the end of the sessions. Everyone skews the truth to give management an ego massage. The relevant measures and instruments are all missing. What did you really get for the money and the time?

Chapter Forty-Five

Chapter 45: Medicating the Dead

Cosmetic company advertisements for hair care products have, in some instances, mystified me and I used at least one example in some of the psychology classes I've taught. What was it that caught my eye as particularly odd, unscientific or just plain contrary to common sense? How about "nourishing" your hair? The hair is dead, never to benefit from nourishment again once it breaks out of the scalp to adorn our wonderful pates. The portion of the hair that is living is found beneath the scalp, and I seriously doubt it requires cosmetic nourishment.

So, what the companies are doing is telling us to apply products to cause hair's rather rough shafts to bend or lie flat to give that wonderful, silky look we cherish. Problem hair has been the bane of many a person's day or has thwarted their efforts to look well-groomed.

So, feed the hair and get on with your wonderful life. I'm sure it has sold a ton of product. But it never breathed life into those dead cells.

Advertising is meant to make products appealing, and I fully understand their intent and how they go about utilizing those oh-so-well-honed steps on Maslow's ladder of motivation. This despite the fact that Maslow has been found wanting in his theory, but we'll just leave that to the academics to consider at great length while the B-schools go on droning about his wonders and how to apply the theory to business. How well did the steps apply to Maslow himself? Not hard to find out once you read a biography of his life ("The Right to Be Human"). He had his personal challenges, too, but I don't believe he fully explored how he had molded his motivational theory to meld with his personal demons.

Today, once again, my mail directed me to an article that, if not shocking, was laughable and just more than a shade laughable than feeding dead hair. The article? How about Medicare continuing to pay for 348 expensive prescription medications for people who were already dead? The Medicare program, it seems, has a rule that they continue to pay for prescriptions for 32 days after someone's death. Does that make any sense to anyone? What would that 32-day supply be used for? Certainly it wouldn't help the intended beneficiary. And this discovery after a scouring of a small sample of Medicare cases was only scratching the surface. The true enormity of the problem has yet to be revealed, if ever. Oh, bills were not submitted by pharmacies in a timely manner? That might work.

The great minds at Medicare assume the medications were then diverted to simple street sales and converted into cash at all of our expense. Some or many someones were reaping the benefits of someone's death and not just from life insurance payments. Calling this particular fillip in the program incompetence doesn't come near enough to the words I would prefer to use here.

How do you write and review a program that permits prescription payments after a person is dead? Let's see how many reasons for this you can conjure up. I can't think of one except the fact that someone was asleep at the wheel when they were supposed to read these regulations for logic. But, of course, we do know that many bills pass through Congress without ever having been read by our legislators, who then vote on them. Knowing this, the minions of whoever carefully construct paragraphs to meet their particular motivation. It's Maslow in action, but which step was that on the ladder?

Long live the dead, and long may they rule in this most chaotic of motivational universes.

Chapter 46: Isn't It Curious That...?

One of the greatest assets for any living thing, be it human or animal, is curiosity. It is the basis of extraordinary creations, and there's one simple thing you need to do to nurture it in yourself. We read all the time about procedures to enhance our curiosity, how to produce greater creativity in ourselves, and all manner of programs and tricks overflowing our mail and the vast trove of electronic media available to us.

How many times this week alone have you been bombarded with yet another surefire way to get that old creativity machine lying unused in the recesses of your brain to burst into new life? Don't they offer new ways to expose your hidden abilities, practice methods to use, or a simple step-by-step recipe that will surely make you into a newer you? Of course you have. All of us want someone to give us that golden formula that will mean we'll be able to crank up and spit out wonderful stuff, whatever it is, from a new, stunningly useful app to a bestseller or a blockbuster film. We all want it.

Years ago, while doing some reading for a course I was taking at the time, I came across an article by someone who was new to me. He was a neurobiologist (stick with me here) who appeared to be breaking new ground in theorizing about the basis of some of our behaviors. Actually, he was wondering why there seemed to be a relationship with certain behaviors or disorders in left-handed persons. The rule he used for himself, and which I have come to adapt for myself, is to see two things that might have a relationship after I note something similar in each. For me, once it happens, it seems so simple and obvious that I can't believe others haven't seen it.

Then I begin to ask what he did, and it is, "*Isn't it curious that...*" and the "that" part is where the magic lies. You feel as though you are beginning the equivalent of an investigation with all the skill of a detective solving a crime. But there's no crime here. There is a mystery, and the key may lie in your hands just as it lay in the hands of others who have failed to ask that simple question that began that journey for truth.

Who was this genius and theoretical "mentor" of sorts to whom I refer? None other than the incomprehensible Dr. Norman Geschwind. Yes, the name may be very new to you, and you may want to stifle a yawn right about now, but you're also curious regarding what he did and if you can, somehow, use that technique for what you do in your life. Yes, you can.

Before his premature death in 1984, Geschwind felt he had unlocked the mystery regarding a few things that seemed to be specific to left-handedness, and, in fact, there was a Geschwind Syndrome. Forget about all the pejoratives we use for those who are left-handed. Did you know that the word sinister comes from the Latin or French word sinistre for left? But we see it as malevolent and representative of evil, don't we? How difficult it is to be one of those people in a decidedly right-handed world where even surgical instruments are primarily made for the right-handed.

What were the features of this syndrome? They included, according to Geschwind's original studies with Dr. Peter Behan, unusual brain development that was clear to anyone looking at brain scans. But no one had really explored what that difference might mean in the lives of these people. Geschwind, taking a page from Louis Pasteur's "*In the fields of observation, chance favors the prepared mind,*" decided to see how that might play out. He found learning disabilities, stuttering, migraine headaches, and autoimmune diseases, like ulcerative colitis, myasthenia gravis and celiac disease, seemed to be inordinately tied to those who were left-handed. Other, later, researchers found problems with his conceptualization of such a connection, and it began a few rounds of neurobiology polo with much back and forth before his death and since.

The syndrome may or may not exist, but what Geschwind has provided for all of us who now know of him and his work is that you begin with that simple question of, "*Isn't it curious that...*" and then you work your way from there to new explorations. Happy hunting.

Chapter Forty-Seven

Chapter 47: An Abundance of Goodies

Artists, writers, photographers and anyone doing research for projects that will include illustrations from our long-gone past are in for the equivalent of an overburdened feast. What's more, the feasting is encouraged, and all of it is free, unless specified otherwise with some small caveats. This trove of potential for the creative or those who just plain want to explore intellectually is yours for the asking. A few clicks and you're in the Internet version of nirvana, and it's called **The Internet Archive.**

I've used some of the material there in the past while involved in writing projects, and, yes, the current website design layout is very dated in appearance. But don't let the exterior mislead you and turn you off to the potential within. A major facelift is in the offing, so stick with the look and continue to see beyond it. In fact, the current curator has incredible plans for the future, and it is truly mind-boggling in scope.

A bit of the size of the current archive can be appreciated when you consider that it has 435 billion web pages, 7 million texts (books), 2.1 million audio recordings, and 1.8 million videos. Want a sample of what's on the site? How about "*The Internet's Own Boy*" about **Aaron Swartz**, the genius who, under pressure from authorities, committed suicide? You can download it free in a number of formats or at **YouTube: https://www.youtube.com/watch?v=9vz06QO 3UkQ&rco=1**.

By anyone's measure, it's a hefty collection with something for everyone, and it's growing thanks to new technology that will permit scanning and collection at other sites. Portability has meant the potential for enormous additions at a fraction of the time and expense.

Only a truly visionary librarian such as Brewster Kahle could have seen the possibilities in the World Wide Web in the early 1990s. That is true creativity. Often, it's the task of dreamers and the adventurous who make the mental breakthroughs that bring wonderful new light to things we could only dream of. Thank you, Mr. Kahle, you have provided an incredible service to the world, and I know there are many who will sing your praises.

As for myself, I remember sitting in my office with my spanking new, portable IBM laptop, which prompted remarks about what it was, what it did and a few somewhat cautious concerns about whether it was going to record conversations or video discussions. It was still rudimentary, but not as it had been when I had one of the first Franklin computers. You may recall they were successfully put out of business by Apple, who sued them for copyright infringement.

I marveled at the FTP connections with foreign countries (no icon-based desktop yet) and connecting to the University of Illinois computer programs site. When the spinning globe indicated I had successfully gotten into, if only marginally, a new interface, Mosaic from Marc Andreessen, it was one of those heart-skip moments. I was IN! I was on that new thing called the web! It was awesome even if I couldn't get the globe to keep spinning and the interface didn't come up at all. I couldn't wait to contact, via FTP, people all over the world. I was communicating with Brazil, Germany, and the UK, and it was glorious!

The feeling must be what it's like to step onto that glass observation point over the Grand Canyon. You feel as though you're stepping into space, and it's totally unknown, and you've never had this experience before, so you can't accurately gauge it. But it's exciting. It must have been the same with anyone who had one of the original shortwave radios. Truly a wonderful experience.

I learned the simple commands, downloaded free programs and waited for the next turn of events. When an icon-based system came into being, it would be years before I knew that Xerox had created it and sold it without ever seeing where its true value lay. Of course, now I expect more, and the Internet Archive has provided a piece of that "more," but I still want more, and I know it's coming.

I don't want games. I want immersive experiences made possible by imaginative programmers who use virtual keyboards or hand/eye commands, making the web now accessible to all for all our senses, not just the visual. I want touch and sound experiences from afar, and I look forward to them and to **The Internet Archive** collecting all of them for me and for generations to come.

Long live the new library in all its formats. It's a far cry from that beautiful wood-paneled library of my childhood where the librarians read stories to us, but it's just as special and inviting.

Chapter 48: The Art of the Hidden Message

A ladybug keeps trying to set up a cozy spot for the cold winter nights ahead, and this little creature has decided that my living space is the exact perfect place for it to be. I've tried at least three times to carefully scoop it up with a paper towel, making a little basket to catch it as I inch the paper along the wall beneath it and then bringing a bit of the top over it until it falls into the scoop. It's delicate work because, while I want the little bug out, I don't want to harm it. Out the window I toss it, but it keeps coming back. Such determination, or maybe it's just opportunity that it sees.

All of this might be a metaphor for things that go on around us every day, and it really hit home tonight as I, in my determination not to get caught up in election returns, watched a few "House of Cards" episodes. Incredible how my efforts toward the ladybug and the congressman's actions on the Hill are so similar. We both want our way. I don't want harm, and maybe he doesn't either, but he's capable of it when he deems it necessary.

The mix of politically themed TV shows should more appropriately be called a rash of shows with the same theme. It's the "Bonanza" of this season, but there are more wily people here than you would find on the Ponderosa in a decade. Straight shooters have gone the way of pull chains in bathroom plumbing, and the new batch of characters has to spend endless nights trying to outfox each other. Just following the machinations can be taxing, but it's also a veritable chess game that draws you in as you watch the moves that are or are not anticipated. The endgame is, of course, taking over the board with your perspicacity.

I can't help but wonder how much of the plots border on what the writers have heard or been fed by people in the know in Washington, DC. Is there really a cleanup woman who is so totally adept in any messy situation that she knows exactly what to do to get the desired result? That, of course, would be "Scandal." I have seen at least two episodes and haven't become a fan. Maybe I just can't swallow that absence of disbelief that is so necessary to liking these shows.

Watching "Breaking Bad," I became a critic of too many "fade to black" scene changes and then an extraordinary action that was never explained. For example, how did Walter White get that ricin into the sugar substitute packet so that he could kill that woman? The man is a genius magician besides being more than a top-notch chemist/meth cook.

I saw a bit of "Madam Secretary," but that didn't catch me, either. Yes, the clothes fit so well, and everyone is so smooth that it's irritating, and they live in such great places. Sure, that's what it's really like, isn't it? After all, the then-current Senate Majority Leader did live at the Ritz-Carlton in Washington, DC and those are some pretty nice digs. I've stayed there on at least one occasion and on another at their hotel in Laguna Niguel, California. Luxurious. What a background for skullduggery.

What I think just might be the value in these shows is that they provide us with a great understanding of just how to be really successful at being underhanded. I'm sure that comes in real handy in business these days and even in education, where you might want to wheedle your way into a cushy administration slot. But then, this was all anticipated years ago with "The Peter Principle," where even the truly mediocre rise to the top by virtue of just staying put. I have seen examples of this. But I've also seen the unbelievably ruthless get to positions of power by cutting everyone else off at the knees, so to speak. They do it so cleverly that the victims never see it coming or, if they do, they know they are powerless to do anything to stop it. The groundwork has been carefully laid, as it always is by Congressman Frank Underwood in Cards.

We can see the shows as entertainment, or we can see them as training. Those looking for seminars on how to bring Sun Tzu into business will find them instructive as well as entertaining. So, you don't have to read and re-read "The Prince" or "The Art of War" in order to learn guile. Just watch TV and be sure to absorb all the hidden messages.

Wonder if the ladybug will be back tomorrow.

Chapter 49: Stifling the Genius Within

Genius has always fascinated us, and there is a surfeit of myths associated with it. In my childhood, there was a disheveled African-American man who wandered our neighborhood talking to himself. He never bothered anyone, never asked for anything, just walked in a seemingly aimless manner. The popular agreement in the area was that he had cracked under the strain of college, and what we saw was the unhappy result. Did this truly happen to him, or did he have schizophrenia? It does usually begin to make itself evident during the latter part of high school or the first two terms in college. But no one knew anything about him or where this belief had started and by whom.

Other examples of genius can be found in many of the incredibly accomplished and heralded actors we've come to know as true icons of the silver screen. Some of them have spent multiple stints in psychiatric hospitals; others found the lack of understanding that they faced day after day, and they chose to end it all. The tortured genius is another myth.

Bipolar disorder, in one of its stages, seems to be present in many successful professionals. The disorder not only gives them enormous abilities to expend inordinate energy for more hours than the rest of us, but they can, eventually, burn themselves out. I've been told by patients with the disorder that the reason they don't want to take the meds, which serve to calm them down, is that it destroys the pleasurable, creative high they experience.

You've heard the often expressed belief that genius and madness are just a shade apart, and professionals flock to seminars each year hoping to get greater insight into this dichotomy. How should a bipolar genius be treated if, in fact, they should be treated, and how to help preserve the creativity and genius while maintaining the person in a less-tortured state? It is no easy task, but the question remains whether the disorder is a manifestation of the extraordinarily talented and creative or just a symptom of an illness, albeit one that does have its positive side.

Now, a new look is being taken by mental health professionals with regard to a disorder that has become the disorder du jour, Attention Deficit Hyperactivity Disorder. The disorder has morphed from ADD (Attention Deficit Disorder) to ADHD or some variant of it. Primarily diagnosed in children and treated with amphetamine medications in the belief that the brains of these kids act in a paradoxical fashion when given these "speed me up" medications, it is now attaining greater attention and being more frequently diagnosed in adults. The new approach may be that these kids and adults were born to explore and find the tedium of school and even some work situations intolerable.

But ADHD, whether a valid assessment of this disorder in children or adults, is also being viewed from a different perspective. Not seen as an inability to attend, but rather a distaste for activities that limit individual curiosity and talent, it may be at a turning point. Squirming may be a way to obtain relief from boredom rather than a deficit to be controlled. Isaac Asimov never worked on one book at a time. He was busy writing at least nine at a time in order to keep himself stimulated. He dropped one and turned to another when the mood struck him, and that happened on a daily basis.

A similar turnaround in another disorder may also receive new appreciation for its value rather than its deficits, and that is Asperger's Syndrome. The latter individuals show specific behaviors that set them apart from others; they may also be socially isolative as a means of focusing all their attention on a specific task. Social skills are not their big suit.

Was Aaron Swartz, the incredible computer coding genius who created RSS and code for Wikipedia before there was a Wikipedia, someone with Asperger's? Good question. He did have incredible abilities. Watch the documentary "The Internet's Own Boy" to fully gain an appreciation of what he achieved in his short life.

Should we reconsider our professional approaches to individuals with one of these "disorders" if, in fact, they are truly in need of prescription medications to somehow contain these symptoms? Or, are we medicating something that should be approached from a totally different perspective? The voices will be raised on both sides of this argument, I'm sure, because there are many vested interests that will be shaken in terms of their power and certain monetary aspects related to treatment.

Were Thomas Edison and Leonardo da Vinci in need of treatment for their sleep disorders? If they had been medicated, would we have had the wonder of their creations? Two decades ago, an insightful psychiatrist wrote about medicating out our personalities, and he may have been more right than he realized.

Antidepressants may be absolutely essential in some cases, but in others the smoothing that occurs may be a distortion of the individual's potential. The lobotomy never did what Dr. Walter Freeman (famous for golden ice pick surgery) claimed it would, and it probably did more harm than good. Consider that there are many "strait jackets" that are not quite literally jackets at all, but they do the same thing; they inhibit, restrict and frustrate. They are, if you will, a type of punishment for the different.

Food for thought regarding labeling and diagnosing when a diagnosis may not be what is needed.

Chapter 50:
Where Hospitals
Fail

Y ou've been in a hospital either for treatment or to visit a friend
    or even to volunteer at some activity, I suspect. And you've been
around a lot of hospital treatment rooms, waiting areas, lavatories and
spoken to personnel. The assumption you make is that everything is
kept shipshape and all the appropriate infection control rules are being
followed and someone is always on the lookout. It seems you would
be quite wrong in that assumption, and the latest horrific incidents in
Dallas regarding Ebola seem to give this statement credibility.

But, you say, you haven't been in a hospital that is in the midst of
an Ebola incident, so you're okay. Well, let's look a bit more closely
at this, and I'll relate what I've noticed, and you can add what you've
noticed and what you've read.

The Dallas hospital held a dramatic press conference as soon as
they knew they had an Ebola patient, but they were really premature

with their information. They either didn't have all the information or they didn't look closely enough to get it. Either way, they first blamed a nurse who failed to properly complete an Ebola checklist with Mr. Duncan. Then, they next slid the blame over to software glitches where two different systems didn't communicate information to everyone involved. So, first it was the nurses (and aren't they the first to be blamed all the time?), then it was that darned technology, and now it seems it's something else.

Watch enough of the TV news, and you'll be able to piece together the following:

1. there's a blood test that could be used to identify persons at risk of developing Ebola but there's not doing this

2. the protective gear or the procedures used for decontamination is inadequate. The gear used in West Africa is much more sophisticated and was used by the CDC Director Tom Frieden when he visited an African hospital. Not so in Texas. In Texas they had to use duct tape to close the openings on the neck area of their protective outfits because the suits didn't fit properly.

3. training to be used in instances of infectious diseases has lagged behind the times

4. protocols are full of holes, e.g., not keeping track of everyone who could have been exposed from the very first moment a patient came in

5. a lack of fully qualified medical leadership seems to be lacking. A judge, while willing and intelligent, is no substitute for a medical authority. The CDC has to be "invited" to come into a hospital to help. They are powerless at the moment.

All of this has brought only one thing to the fore, and that's that, in times of serious, potential viral outbreaks, there needs to be a major wake-up call sounded. The bad news, however, isn't this but that hospitals are sloppy in their daily attention to infection control and cleanliness even without Ebola being present. Allow me to give you a few illustrations of what I've noted on cursory and casual observation while in a few major hospitals where interns and residents are trained and which are affiliated with world-class medical centers.

One exam room in an ER (now referred to as the ED) had at least one major breach of infection/sterility control. Tubing to be used in procedures, which was packaged in sealed plastic pouches, was stored on a rod on a rack. In order to store it there, the packaging was pierced, thereby canceling any hint of sterile supply. Dust was also noted on cabinets and the floor. The small lavatory next to this room had blood on the wall, which had not been cleaned.

On a patient floor, one of the lavatories had feces on the wall. The rooms are turned much like the tables in a coffee shop, and thorough cleaning and inspection seem to be overlooked. In the radiology department, where people with all manner of illnesses are screened, dust bunnies floated under the instrument tables, and a layer of dust was on the fire extinguisher and window sills.

The chairs in the capacious waiting room were stained. The CT scan machine, where a patient with a hacking cough had just been scanned, was not cleaned before another patient was to be scanned.

At another hospital, where they do pulmonary function testing, the tubing used by patients to blow into the machine is not changed or cleaned until the end of the day. How is this infection control? I didn't see a change in the mouthpiece, either, between patients. An enclosed pod-like unit, where other pulmonary testing was performed, had noticeable dust on the interior surfaces. On the interior surfaces where persons with lung conditions were seated!

The door leading to an isolation unit for persons with respiratory disorders had a large sign on it, "To be closed at all times," yet it was latched open for the several hours that I had an opportunity to view it.

This happened on the same day that the hospital was having a JCAHO (Joint Commission on Accreditation for Healthcare Organizations) inspection for their continuing accreditation. How did they miss this one? Or were they carefully directed to other areas? Curious.

At a back service door at a major hospital, a body in a bag was strapped on a gurney, and no one appeared to be in attendance. Was it a mortuary pick-up, and, in any case, why wasn't someone there with it?

Hospitals are obviously not doing a good job in many areas of sanitation and infection control. Is this the reason that there is such a problem with sepsis infections? How many people are monitoring their infection control at each hospital, and are they getting a bit too casual with their protocols? One major example, like that in Dallas, isn't just a wake-up call; it's a thundering boom that should be reverberating off the walls of every healthcare organization in this country and the world.

How careful is your hospital when it comes to their procedures? You might want to look around next time you're there and, perhaps, take a few cell phone photos for the administration.

Chapter 51: Who Owns the Research You Paid For?

Academia would have an extremely difficult time existing and running the many research projects for which it gains fame and attracts the most brilliant minds in each discipline if it were not for that golden cache called "grants." Grants make the academic and the research world run smoothly and provide a very nice living for a few and gainful employment for the many who wish to attain the heights of the few. In this pursuit of that lofty position, teams work feverishly on writing grants for weeks, if not months, at full tilt almost 24 hours a day to produce exactly what the grant indicates it has been made available for in terms of research.

Some grants are very specific, and few can snag that golden goose, but there is a wellspring of grants produced by the U.S. government in all its many departments, and these are sought mightily. Take a moment out to just give a quick scan at the first page of any published study that has been funded by one of these grants, and, at the very bottom, you will see which agency forked over the money.

Now give a bit of thought to what the federal government says about this material. If a study has been produced with this funding, which is your and my money, we all get to use it and we don't have to pay any fees. Some agencies will tell you that, if you'd be so kind, they would really appreciate a credit line somewhere in your product that lists the agency as the grantor. All of it is published by the Government Printing Office.

There is no copyright protection for these materials, and they may be freely used. Ah, but there's a glitch here. Professional publishing, so I understand, is a multi-billion dollar business. The material published, in large measure, is the product of researchers working under federal grants. So, why do the researchers give up any rights they may have to the material if, in fact, they had any rights at all? As I understand it, they wouldn't have any rights. Then how does a publisher get rights from someone who doesn't have the power to hand them over? All very peculiar.

I started thinking about this as I began to watch, once again, "The Internet's Own Boy," the inspiring but tragic story of Aaron Swartz, computer genius and the advocate of RSS (real simple syndication) and the creative commons use agreement. The Creative Commons, or CC as it is sometimes referenced, allows material to be freely used by anyone with some specific caveats by the author. But not always. Some authors would rather allow it to go into the wild as it were and let anyone have it for any purpose at all. But I still don't think they're thinking anyone's going to use their material to make money off them in some sneaky, underhanded dealings.

On the Creative Commons U.S. website, it states:

"Creative Commons licenses help creators retain copyright while allowing others to copy, distribute, and make some uses of their work, at least non-commercially. The CC License choice provides an easy way for creators to define the terms on which others may use their work."

There can be exceptions in the license as it indicates, but that is up to the author, who may place the work in the public domain, if they wish, so that it is free to be used by anyone, but not for anyone to use and then get their own copyright on the material. The general idea is that knowledge should be freely shared and not trapped by a paywall whenever someone is working on a project that could benefit from the inclusion of this material. Knowledge expansion should be the goal, not lucre-creep.

College instructors already have something called "fair use," which means that materials may be reproduced specifically for a class. The instructor does not have to pay for this use or even, it's my understanding, request permission to use it in this manner. Some professors did get into trouble with this many years ago when they regularly reproduced materials into class packets that students had to purchase either at the college bookstore or a reproduction service near the college. One of the schools was a university where I received one of my degrees, and I was one of those students buying those packets.

Consider how truly ludicrous it is that taxpayers should pay for research and then someone should come along, snag the material and offer it for sale as though it were their intellectual property solely by virtue of their publishing it in their journal. I thought journals were supposed to turn out their own material, not cadge articles from researchers (who desperately need to "publish or perish"). Aren't subscriptions the means of making money in journal publishing? If you've ever written anything that needed a bit of scientific referencing in it and you wanted to read the original published article, you were quickly awakened to the fact that these articles are available, but at a price. Government printing office articles, pamphlets, booklets, etc., are free and free of copyright.

And the price of journal articles can be pretty steep. Sometimes it's up over $40 just for a few pages, and suppose you need more than one article. Suppose you need 10 or more; why should you buy all those articles for which you have already paid with your tax money? Should you be yelling at your Congressman or Senator? Maybe because they have made much of this possible, it would seem.

Those whose hearts are with the movement to open up the bars surrounding research are working to make information more freely available. You can keep up with what they are doing at the website: Open Educational Resources. Recently, in fact, I took a course with a professor who had written the textbook for the course, and he made it freely available on the Internet under a Creative Commons license, which made it wonderful for thousands of students all around the world—it was an Internet course in computing.

Aaron Swartz may have been hounded, persecuted and, ultimately, driven to believe that life was no longer worth the struggle, but his beliefs live on. We will all benefit, but at what a price for him. RIP Aaron Swartz, you fought the good fight for all of us. It may not have been in the most palatable fashion for some, but you never realized the forces against you and the motivation of others for power that would drive you to hang yourself.

Chapter Fifty-Two

Chapter 52: There Must Be a Pony

Metaphors and simple stories have extreme power to influence our thinking and our perception of not only things around us but also of ourselves. If you'd like to dip your toe into the wonderful world of metaphor, read one of the works of Dr. Milton Erickson, "My Voice Will Go with You," and you will soon see the uses of this form of subtle communication.

Erickson was, at one time in his life, afflicted with what sounds like polio, and it left him unable to move from a wheelchair or to use his hands. Determined to help himself, he worked and struggled each day to move just one finger. Once he achieved that goal, he went on to increase the movement he had, and, finally, he did manage to regain some movement, but he never left his wheelchair. It was at this time that he decided that the power of the mind could be brought under control in order to achieve change in one's life, and he utilized unique metaphors, which he constructed for his patients. After his death, the technique became a tool for a number of his students who continue to use it today in their own books on the subject. BTW, the color purple is always associated with Erickson.

How often have we used tales of exotic places to teach our children lessons for life that may not seem like lessons at all? It's the same with we adults. We can learn valuable lessons in what seems like a flash, and sometimes, it can even be done with humor or incredible simplicity.

A good example of the simplicity form can be found in that of-ten-told story of the prince and the pony. It's been reformulated in a number of different settings, but the message is the same. As I heard it, it goes like this:

A young prince was unhappy because nothing seemed to be hap-pening that was lifting his spirits. Why he was feeling this way is never discussed, but a wise man in his court knew how to help him and to bring the laughter and positive attitude back to his way of thinking. So, he arranged to have the prince come into a room where one door remained closed, and as the prince faced the door, the wise man had him open it. Looking at what was on the other side of the door, the prince saw a huge mound of horse droppings. Initially, he was perplexed, but then the light came back to his eyes, and he shouted, "There must be a pony!"

The moral of the story? Even when things don't appear to be very positive, you can turn it around and see the possibility of something wonderful, but initially hidden to you. It's another example of "*What the mind does not know, the eye does not see*." So, look and seek the secrets that lie within.

It's a simple way of conveying a very important lesson about placing a positive perspective on almost anything. Metaphors are power, and the underlying message may not be immediately apparent, so allow it to percolate a bit, and it will rise to the top of your awareness if you permit it.

Where are the messages you've missed today? Take another look.

Chapter 53: The Most Frightening Words You Never Want to Hear

No, it's not something like "Of all the things of mice and men, these are the things that might have been" or something to that effect. True, the things that might have been can send us musing and regretting for too much of our time if we let them. But you have no idea what the most frightening words are until you are in a situation where they will turn your body cold, bring a sweat to your forehead, and make your heart race with fear. Pray you never hear them.

How do I know what they are? Because I used them, and they had the effect I wanted. No, I'm not a sadist, nor do I admire the Marquis de Sade or his penchant for acts against little children, but a little bit of fear can go a long way. I needed those words in order to turn a young man around so he'd begin to have some vision of how terrible his existence could be if I chose to do what I was empowered to do.

The words were something that have lived in my memory since the first time I used them some 25 years ago on a weekday morning in a small cinder block room with a table bolted to the floor. Why do they come to mind now? Sometimes memories bubble up from those neuronal depths because a little jog, a short phrase or a bit of video pulls them back in full force. Today I was watching an episode of "Orange Is the New Black." Yes, TV dramas can have qualities we don't always attribute to them. They can bring new insights, if they're well framed and written, and they can serve as more than entertainment. But not for everyone.

The scene in question is from Season One, where Pipper is put into the shoe (solitary confinement) because the social worker on her unit can't handle his lesbian preoccupation, sexual frustration with his wife, or the fact that he has too much power. He's a snake who tries, oh, so hard to keep that aspect of his personality hidden beneath that wonderful professional demeanor he affects.

Enough time in an environment of sensory deprivation will change you, no matter what you think that you would be able to endure. The research studies have shown what it can do, and, certainly, we know that the CIA has made frequent use of these techniques and others that are a bit more violent. The silence can be so bad that, like those put into water tanks, the sound you hear is that of your heart beating. Watch the Dirk Bogarde film "*The Mind Benders*" and get a feel for what it might be like.

We've all had a bit of this fear reaction. Remember what it was like when you were a kid playing the game known as "Hide & Seek?" You hid somewhere, trying hard not to breathe in any perceptible way so that the seeker wouldn't find you, and you prayed you'd be safe in your hiding place. Many times you weren't caught, and even if you were, what was the worst that would happen? Yeah, you' wouldn't win the game. There weren't any horrible consequences.

But in the TV series, the man teases Pipper with those frightening words. And they are, "**I have the keys**." Not too scary, you say? No, not unless you're on the receiving end of being confined and helpless and have no way to get anyone to be an ally or to help in any way. Then it becomes very, very frightening, especially if you're young and vulnerable and you've never been in a place like this before.

When did I use the words, and why? I was working on an admissions unit in a psychiatric hospital, and I was told that a new admission was coming in. The admission was a 21-year-old male who had gotten very drunk the night before, had a fight with his girlfriend, and threatened to kill himself. I have no idea why he wasn't held in a bed at a local hospital or overnight in the local jail. Whatever the reason, he was coming to us, and I was to be the responsible person to evaluate him. It was my decision: admit or have him taken home.

They brought him in wearing handcuffs and looking a little bit scared. He was trying hard to just keep from trembling, and I knew from his history and the events of the prior night that I could make a difference in this kid's life if I used the words. But mind you, it's not only the words; it's an explanation of what the words portend.

After the initial evaluation, when I had determined he wasn't suicidal nor was he an appropriate admission for a psychiatric hospital, I began. First I told him that three locked doors separated him from freedom once I took him inside. Then I gave a rather abbreviated but nonetheless explicit description of where he would be sleeping with 30 or so psychiatric male patients behind yet another thick wooden locked door. "*The staff will all be on the other side of that door,*" I said, "*and they won't hear what's happening in that room where they've just left you, and I don't want to describe what could happen in there. It could be pretty ugly, and since the staff are not only on the other side of that heavy door and separated by yet another door with a large day room in between, you could experience something you really don't want to happen to you.*"

Then I initiated my major bit of theatrics as I pulled my large ring of 20 keys from the chain that attached it to my waist and slammed it on the desk in front of him. Yes, I know "Seven Beauties" is dancing through your head right about now. He flinched, and I told him, "*You don't want me taking you back there, do you? I have the keys, you see. Once I take you there, I have no power over what happens back there.*"

He shook his head, and his eyes opened wide as he muttered that he didn't mean what he said. He was drunk. His girl had upset him, and he wanted to go home. End of story.

I signaled the front desk to have someone pick him up and take him home. We never saw him at that hospital again, and I suspect he wanted to stay very far away because I had the keys and he didn't.

Chapter 54: Digitally Illiterate But Able to Learn

The digital age has been around long enough for most of us to be at least minimally acquainted with the lingo, but apparently that isn't so. I had a telling illustration of this today via a chance interaction in a store. Allow me to expound on this.

While waiting for my package to be prepared, I overheard a conversation between an elderly man and the man behind the counter. The store is one of those that provide not only shipping services but also fax preparation, computers for preparing short documents, and assorted tools to prepare small booklets. It's a great all-in-one spot for some people, but for others it is a place of confusion no matter the efforts to help.

I heard the discussion as the man was first directed to the correct paper weight for his intended use (he had selected a too-heavy stock for a laser printer), then a blank look came over his face and that of the guy behind the counter. What caused this absolute lack of connection?

The man had written a book some years ago, had it printed at this shop, and now wanted to revise it. Simple, right? No, not simple at all. Receiving no solution for his quandary, he wheeled on his heel and began to head for the door as I stepped forward. Never having been a Girl Scout, I am, nevertheless, willing to offer help when I can. I thought I might be able to help him.

I began with a simple question. "*What is it that you want to do with your book*?" He looked at me as though I had just broken into his home but stopped and briefly explained he wanted to revise his book. "*They're telling me that I have to scan all the pages and then revise it, but I can't do that.*" My next question was pretty elementary. "*What type of software are you using?*"

"*Software? I don't know anything about that.*" I explored a bit more. "*What digital format is your book in, and what do you want to do with it? Perhaps make it into an ebook?*"

"*Now you're way over my head,*" he explained with no hint of a smile on his face. "*I don't know what scanning is or how to scan it. I don't know what to do.*" I tried to offer some suggestions about how his dilemma might be resolved, but he wouldn't hear any of it. His mind was made up. He lived in this world of computerized activity, and he didn't even know what "digital" meant.

"*I guess I'll just have to go back and retype the entire thing,*" he sighed. Well, yeah, I guess that's what he'll have to do, and he probably won't do it with word processing software, and there will be no digital footprint for his next go-round. His work will be an exercise in frustration (constantly revising entire pages on a typewriter) with a hefty dose of anger thrown in for this infernal thing called "documents" and the Internet and things digital.

I can understand how he must have felt. My suggestions were of no use to him, and he left with his ream of 20-pound white paper under his arm with a bit of an angry scowl on his face. He had been undone in his literary efforts by those in charge of the world: the coders, the digital literati and a bunch of kids. It was an impossible situation for him, and I can imagine the beating that typewriter was going to receive once he got back to it.

I'd been naive enough to think that everyone knew how to use a computer and was at least minimally conversant with word processing software. I didn't expect expertise in Excel, PowerPoint, Twitter, YouTube or, heaven forbid, computer coding. The light bulb went off in my head, and now I understand why the local senior centers are presenting basic courses in computer use, and these courses are so painfully simplistic. It was simple because they didn't know anything about computers. Digital was entirely new and unknown to them.

Some were even afraid to turn a computer on because they thought they'd break it or it would jump forward and expect them to give all sorts of elaborate commands, and they were nervous around computers. Yes, afraid. They also felt inadequate and unable to learn this "stuff my grandkids know all about."

My website does have a page on computers where I point people to some simple programs that can be helpful. One of the best places, in my estimation, is YouTube, where you can learn just about anything you need to know. The problem is breaking through that fear connection.

OK, seniors, you conquered cars without heaters or oil filters, you clipped coupons to get meat during WWII, you converted from gas lights to electricity, and you got a checking account. You CAN learn some basic computer operations. Sure, it's effortful, and maybe it's even a bit like learning a foreign language, but just because you're over

70 or so doesn't mean your brain has been put into cold storage. You can learn, and learning will really increase your sense of mastery and even self-esteem.

I guess you could say I'm asking that you show a bit of bravery in this battle of the brains, but you will be rewarded. Learning to read opened worlds of wonder for you when you first went to elementary school, and the computer will do that and more. It isn't a tool for storing recipes. I remember when that was how they pitched computers to women. Recipes? The computer is a time machine with more promise and wonder than I could ever explain to anyone.

Need a GED because you never finished high school because you had to go to work to help support your family? You can do it on the Internet. Thinking of taking a vacation, but you need some ideas about where you might go, what it would cost, and whether or not you'd like it? Yes, again, the Internet is there waiting like some genie in a box for your commands. And the commands are real simple, mostly "Enter" and "Copy and paste." Go for it and be amazed.

Senior citizen doesn't mean it's all over and behind you. The wonder is waiting. Take the first step.

Chapter Fifty-Five

Chapter 55: Sign on the Dotted Line, Please

The dotted (or perhaps not) line has become the place where we are constantly asked to affix our signature attesting to the fact that we are agreeing with all that appears above it. Do we carefully review all that text, and do we know that we can make changes to it before signing? How many times have you signed where directed, never read the document, and didn't request a copy for your files? I will bet you've done it more than you care to admit.

The tragic death of Joan Rivers is one sad illustration regarding forms used to permit a medical procedure. But the one thing that apparently was missing when the procedure actually went ahead was that someone failed to follow the specifics of the signed form. There was limited permission given for a very specific procedure, which was completed and nothing else was to have been performed.

The media are reporting that additional medical probing was finished, and a biopsy may have been attempted. The current investigative findings include unauthorized procedures, unauthorized personnel performing the procedures, and a number of either contradictory actions or a lapse in protocols prior to sedating patients. The legal process will sort out this particular case, but it is instructive for all of us.

Healthcare providers utilize a variety of forms prior to any evaluations or treatments, and this provides some degree of protection for the patient as well as the healthcare professional and the facility where the procedure is to be initiated. Within the many paragraphs of text are a few items that most patients gloss over and never notice. Hospital admissions, in particular, may be unnerving tests of your resolve to do everything with complete care. Among the forms to be signed will, assuredly, be some form of permission given to do whatever without first asking, once again, for permission. You've granted them complete authority.

Are you aware that when you sign one of the permission documents for evaluation or treatment, there are rights you have signed away? One of the rights is privacy, where you agree that the professional may video, take specimens or other materials, and use these for research, training or presentations. With your signature on that bottom line, you may find your case appearing in a journal, book or video presentation on YouTube.

You can, if you wish, cross out this section, affix your initials to it and date the deleted section. This should maintain your rights, but if you are fully sedated, how do you know what will happen? In the case of Joan Rivers, we hear someone in the room began to take cell phone photos. It may or may not be true. We leave that to the attorneys.

Some forms may indicate that you've relinquished your rights to your intellectual property (photos, videos or text) once you upload it to someone's server. This permission is often on internet sites, and you "approve" or "agree" with that little check mark and then log in to the site. You've just bought the farm.

In the case of photos, you can go into the metadata and place your name and copyright information. Even this bit of privacy protection isn't as robust as we'd like, and the data doesn't migrate if someone were to do a screen grab or copy the image from the web. Watermarks might help, but they distort the image when it appears in any format. You can remove it if the potential user notifies you of their interest in your photo or video. Text, on the other hand, is totally at risk except when it is copied and pasted from certain Internet sites because the underlying HTML may go along with it. But even here there are ways to cadge the copy and get around the HTML protection that tries to stop right-click-save-as move.

How many rights have you signed away when you complied with that simple request to "Sign here, please"? You'll never know unless you begin carefully reading the text above your valuable signature and amending it as you wish. You never need to give absolute 100% permission to use anything.

Chapter Fifty-Six

Chapter 56: Rape-shaming the Women

Rape is a topic we really don't want to deal with in most instances, but it is a fact of life, and I recall a book, by a feminist leader decades ago, that detailed the history of rape as a tool of submission and another that compared it to the fear of lynchings pervasive in our country at one time. It was never brought up during at the trials in Nuremberg even though it was rampant in the concentration camps. Familiar with the "Lebensborn Program?" Women were used against their will to become vessels for the super race that Hitler wanted to create. How do you create a super race when you're using women you've already denigrated?

What has kept the women from coming forward? To me, that's an indictment right off the bat of any woman who does come forward. She is immediately accused of having some plan to gain either money or to damage someone's reputation or to get her 15 minutes of fame in the media spotlight. Destroy her at all costs would seem to be the mantra because, after all, don't women cry "rape!" all the time, and doesn't "NO" really mean "Yes?" No, it doesn't, and we have to stop this rape-shaming of women.

Now, we are paying new attention to this crime against women (and men). It is more common in college than we wanted to know. I recall a very well-known college making it a point not to tell parents, on those famous parent weekends, about the high incidence of rape on their campus. I don't know how the parents managed to miss the postings near the front doors of buildings that indicated any woman wanting an escort home could call a specific number for one. Who would ordinarily need an escort on this oh-so-famous campus unless there was a clear and present danger that the young women would be raped or disappear? Yes, disappear. Posters around the campus carried the photo of a young woman bicyclist who had disappeared on campus. I don't know if they ever found her.

Suddenly, the military is admitting to somewhat shocking statistics about rape in their ranks and writing it off to better reporting. Doesn't that smack of something more? Say, for instance, that all of this has been happening while they were doing all that wonderful anti-rape training and setting up counseling? So, it's similar to the same argument we saw when women began to get more DUI citations; not more women drinking but more police not letting them get by. Women suffer from alcoholism just as men do, and, yes, it's the reporting that changed. So, I have to think that there's a lot more rape and sexual abuse going on in the military than even these new statistics allude to. *Susan Brownmiller wrote about it in 1975.*

Rape isn't just out in the general population because the not-so-well-hidden secret is that rape is rampant in other places where the victims are like chickens in a pen. Prison isn't just a place anyone is sent to be punished for crimes. It is well-known that it is where they go to be raped with the tacit permission of those in authority. Young people are particularly victimized by prison populations in adult and juvenile facilities, and what is being done about it? To my mind, prisons are places of containment of gangs that prey on the "fresh fish," the innocent, the vulnerable, and the less muscular. Don't think it doesn't happen in women's prisons, too.

Bill Cosby is only one well-known entertainment personality who has been accused by multiple women of having drugged and raped them. In England, now that he's dead, we find that possibly hundreds of children were raped by their beloved well-known performer, Jimmy Savile. The entertainer was active, it would seem, for over 50 years in these heinous acts against children. Parents were duped just as we have been in the case of highly successful entertainers in the US.

Hollywood has long been the capital of filmmaking and licentious lifestyles. Public relations experts, press agents, adept attorneys and studio bosses were well-schooled in keeping the seamier side of Lotus Land hidden from public view. After all, it would affect box office sales, wouldn't it? Forget about the women, the young men and the children whose lives would be destroyed. There was so much collateral damage in the push for the bottom line. Some were no more than mere tissues to be used, abused and thrown aside.

Have we begun to lift up the rock under which these crimes have been hidden? I tend to be cautiously sanguine about all of it. Will money and power prevail, or will social change truly come to bring relief to the survivors? Let's wait and see.

Chapter 57: Physicians and Psychologists Who Need...What?

Physicians need, undoubtedly, help in many areas. Besides their burnout rate and the current issue of vicarious trauma, there are several others. Many of them are engaged in a current turf battle much like that experienced between psychologists, psychiatrists, social workers, counselors and now "coaches" of every stripe. It's always about turf, and it can get pretty ugly as each side tries to gird up its loins for yet another go at the other side. Reminds me of two sumo wrestlers preparing to duke it out in a sand ring. But these rings aren't so circumscribed and obvious. Mostly, they are fought in subtle public relations battles that are aimed at winning the allegiance of new people into the field and fortifying what turf they have.

Aside from the anesthesiologists battling the nurse anesthetists and the nurse practitioners and midwives battling the OB/GYNs, there are the PAs (physician's assistants) trying to find their place in the ranks of health care. Each will probably find comfort in the arms of various insurance plans that will emphasize cost containment at any cost—almost. That is until there's a major lawsuit or some truly horrendous tragedy. Then there will be the "**I told you so**" sayers who will pompously sit on the sidelines feeling pretty pleased with themselves as they stamp those "For deposit only" checks.

One lawsuit, reported in The National Psychologist, noted that someone denied autism treatment for an individual and the establishment of a $6 million fund to reimburse claimants for out-of-pocket expenses resulting from their denied claims. But there's a potentially far-reaching issue of suit, which may have major implications for everyone in psychology and which will be headline-worthy for sure. This issue is currently gaining momentum.

The case in point relates to the psychologists, psychiatrists and medical personnel who aided in or participated in the plan for "enhanced interrogation" used on prisoners at Guantanamo and Abu Ghraib prisons. Cries of foul and actions to change the thinking of those in positions of authority at The American Psychological Association didn't seem to receive the degree of agreement one would expect when the word "torture" comes up in a dialog on ethics and psychologists. One psychologist ran for the office of president of the APA on a platform affirming total disagreement with any psychologist being involved in any form of "enhanced interrogation," aka torture. He didn't win.

Now, when more details have come out, including the payment of over $80M to two psychologists, the topic is a fresh one that requires more action than previously shown by this professional organization. Mind you, APA was pretty much alone in not condemning these actions while the American Psychiatric Association and the American Medical Association took immediate action. Both groups totally banned members from having any role in the utilization or planning of such actions against anyone.

Suddenly, it's time for a thorough review of just what APA did or did not do relative to the issue, and there is to be an internal investigation by a well-respected source, David H. Hoffman, an attorney, who has already begun stretching the parameters of his search for facts. His full report was due sometime by March 2015, and it will be interesting to see what his conclusions are. The two psychologists involved in the government's interrogations are well beyond the reach of the APA since neither is a member any longer, and both have taken their millions and carved out new lives for themselves.

On the physicians' front, and unrelated to the torture, we haven't heard of any truly outrageous behavior save for the Medicare fraud cases that bob up to the surface every few months. Yes, these involve millions and many of them are for improper billing for ghost or unnecessary procedures, "patients" paid to file claims, or overuse of prescription privileges for controlled substances.

What we do not hear is how those in medicine can maintain their level of knowledge and skill without ever having to show some form of verification. Although they may have "verification," it can be pretty dodgy. I've heard of one instance involving at least 15 physicians where continuing education was a matter of sitting in a room once a month and hearing about a type of case unrelated to their specialty. Of course, anyone can make a case for this adding to their competence in some way, but what about education related to their actual specialty?

As diabetes affects more and more adults and children in the United States, there will be a growing need for special knowledge and care related to patients' kidneys. We know that diabetes is a quiet, dreadful killer that affects the heart and the kidneys as well as the nervous system and vision, but we also have learned that residencies in nephrology (the care of kidney conditions) are going begging. Will physicians in internal medicine pick up the slack, and how will consumers know that they are adequately up on the research and treatments? Take their word for it? Not a very wise measure. Depend on drug companies to do continuing education? Not a wise choice, either. The conflict of interest here is much too great.

Then there's the question of physicians who are no longer able to practice because of mental impairments or alcohol/drug abuse. Who weeds them out? In some hospitals I've heard that quite impaired physicians had to have nurses guide them through a routine test to listen with a stethoscope to a patient's heart. In another hospital, a psychiatrist who suffered from alcohol-related cognitive problems actually talked back to the trees outside his hospital. They were taunting him, but no one did anything about it. He had so many car accidents that his car looked like it came from a demolition derby run. The prescription pad was still pushed his way, and he signed off on anything.

Another physician, in a fit of psychotic anger, stabbed himself multiple times in the chest and was admitted to the hospital. When a relative suggested that he needed treatment and should have his license suspended, the attending physician blanched. *"But they'll stop him from practice, and HE'S A PHYSICIAN!"* Do we really want this man out there practicing medicine without making sure he has had adequate treatment for whatever his diagnosis might be?

Many loopholes are in the current system, and, in some states, practitioners are just pushed along to other venues, or their cases get lost in the bureaucracy mill. Sure, like the psychologist who failed to protect a patient from ongoing sexual abuse or the one who, allegedly, shot her husband in the head so she could be with her lover. The latter case is going to trial, I should note.

Any profession has failures and weaknesses, but there are those that must be held to the highest standards, and healthcare stands right up there.

Chapter 58: What's in a Name for a Medical School?

Mornings often bring a plethora of information to me, and I sometimes find it hard to sort out the wheat from the chaff, but today one article in the New York Times, on naming medical schools, struck a responsive chord. It did so because I, too, as an author, found this practice of renaming medical schools after big donors not only onerous but a disservice to the school and those who teach there.

Making billions in whatever industry, the current crop of overly wealthy, fame-seeking individuals is now seeking immortality in one of the only ways they can—getting a school named for them. What have they done to deserve this most special honor? Sure, they opened their checkbooks and probably took a sizable charitable tax deduction for it (does a school naming constitute goods or services for tax purposes?), but how do they come to believe they should have their names plastered on the diplomas of new physicians?

Residency interviewer: "Ah, what medical school did you go to?"

Applicant: "*The Mickey Mouse School of Medicine*, sir."

Residency interviewer: "Ah, fine school and they do such good work in CGI animation."

You can find it laughable if someone demanded that the school (for an incredibly sizable donation) be renamed the "*Hercule Poirot School of Medicine*" or the "*Jacques Clouseau School of Medicine*." The joke, of course, is in knowing who these characters actually are, and these characters are fictional detectives, unlike some real individuals after whom medical schools are named.

These medical school namers, known only to those who follow the WSJ or the stock market, would have no meaning in the context of medical education. But, oh, the grandeur it would impart to the family name! Imagine the delightful dinner parties where you could effortlessly incorporate it into the conversation. Delightful, just delightful. Monsieur Gustave would relish the idea.

This may be the first article I've seen written on the topic, but it isn't the first time I got a bit antsy when I saw something similar on the wall of a hospital Admitting Office. Patients were seated all around the long room with its many clerk alcoves and the circular front desk where everyone had to register.

Behind every single one of those people who were registering was large, bronze lettering on the wall behind them. It couldn't be missed because it was adjacent to the front door. The letter said something like, "*The XYZ Pharmacy* of (name of town where it was located)."

Why was this blatant advertisement for a pharmacy plastered on the wall of the Admissions Office?

Wasn't it a conflict of interest to name a pharmacy right there? Weren't these people going to get prescriptions, and where would they go to fill them? Yes, the XYZ Pharmacy probably, if they didn't have one already. It had to get into their unconscious and stick like glue to come up at some time in the future.

Why not just use the name of the person or family that gave the funds for this hospital addition? Wouldn't that have been more in keeping with the mission of the hospital? Wouldn't that have been the "charitable" thing to do? Ah, remember the parable about the Pharisees and their posturing about giving charity? You don't have to be religious to see the meaning here.

No, money bought that everlasting ad on the wall at this hospital, and it would remain there until, and unless, a new addition was built. Isn't a "charitable" contribution to a nonprofit hospital just dandy? I think it's more of an embarrassment to both the hospital and that pharmacy, but that's me.

What have you seen today that gives you pause? The name sales are on as the one-percenters drive their monikers ever deeper into our culture.

Chapter 59: Design and the Art of Smart

Smart is in, and everywhere we look, things are getting smarter, except they're not. Articles are popping up and telling us the wonders of this new smart world in which we can live. Then they tell us that it's not here yet or we can't afford it, like the smart Google Glasses. But now Google Glass (which was sold to the select few at first for $1,500) is being discontinued. Smart is no longer useful, or what? Are you feeling like the dog that is chasing its tail? I sure am.

How many kids were killed in Sandy Hook school? What type of weaponry was used, and how useful was the school's smart alarm system? The shooter, an avid video game fanatic and intrepid e-mailer to his soon-to-be-deceased mom, didn't need to be and wasn't "smart" in the usual sense, though. His gun could have been smart if it weren't for the paranoia-producing lobby of those who make and sell guns. It's our undeniable right to own dumb guns, isn't it?

And bullets? No, don't make bullets that are smart enough to be identified with specific marks on the casings. Who wants that? The only smart bullets for which there is a current patent are those intended not only to find their target but also to alter course and aid sniper attacks. How about a simple marking that can tell law enforcement where the bullet was bought?

Or does that limit our civil rights to fire guns as we would wish and wherever we wish? Probably would have limited, in some way, the recent shooting death of one woman in a Florida mall and wounding of another by an ex-husband. The man then turned the gun on himself and died. Smart or not?

In this world of smart, it's always a challenge to keep up and see whether smart is just clever, actually has some purposeful use for us, or garners yet more media coverage that is without substance. And, of course, there's always that tagline that grates on the nerves. "But it's not ready right now. You'll have to wait a couple of years."

Years? I have to wait years for this to actually come to fruition? It's like looking at a documentary on the 1939 World's Fair. Are we still waiting for "Futurama" or whatever they were predicting? Didn't Robert Moses take care of all of that when he destroyed the communities in the Bronx in New York and gave us Long Island Levittown gridlock?

Ah, there I go again about the poor media. Will I ever let up on them and their attempts to be clever? No, I never will, so let's put that story to bed. They are still telling us, regularly, about smart cars to prevent drunken driving, aren't they?

But are the auto manufacturers actually making those cars with these safety devices? Nah, not unless you pass a law that they have to have them like seat belts. History buffs might be interested to know that bicycles didn't have brakes until enough people had serious physical injuries. It's where the expression "header" comes from. Now brakes on bikes was smart, I agree.

Car makers would rather we concentrate on smart cars that will drive themselves, not ones that will prevent drunk driving. Which is more likely to have an important impact on the lives of most of us? How many people are killed by drunk drivers each year? How many people will be able to afford driverless cars? Or am I just being an overly educated Luddite, even though that's an oxymoron?

Hooray for design and creativity and all that, but also give us utility and affordability and sustainability. True, that's a demanding yardstick to use, but we must use it because we're losing too much by not adhering to that standard.

Chapter 60: Healthcare and the Medicare Patient

Hospitals seem to be no different from hotels in many instances. In fact, in the well-known hospitals with high national profiles, the hospitals have their own versions of upscale hotels as part of the hospital itself. Go to St. Louis or Chicago and check into certain hospitals and you will be treated and pampered in a private room with room service (cocktails available in many instances), access to a special, gourmet restaurant, and other amenities not usually found in hospitals. It's a real experience that separates the haves from the have-nots. The oil barons and their progeny go to one of these hospitals.

The "haves" have in-room TV with special channels to review any procedures they will have. They can come and go as they please, wear street clothing and chat up a storm in lounges. The "have-nots" on Medicare or with really awful health insurance are put into rooms that aren't too different from those we saw in the 1950s. Staff, too, seem to have a certain bias not only when it comes to coverage but also according to the procedure. Yes, staff are people, too, and they bring all that baggage from outside into their work environment, where they hold sway over what you get, what gets done and how you are spoken to.

Case in point: A woman in her 50s with awful insurance coverage goes into a hospital for a weight-reduction procedure. The patient and the nursing staff were from two different racial groups, and that would be a factor in any experiment, so I mention it here as a possible intervening variable in how this all played out.

The procedure went fine, but hours afterward, in the Recovery Room, the patient complained of severe nausea (a common side effect of the procedure) and had a few simple questions.

Question 1: Can I have something for the pain? Answer: No, because we've already given you morphine, and you have to wait. The patient had already made everyone aware that she could not take morphine since it caused severe vomiting, but they gave it anyway.

Question 2: My arm is swelling up and is hot. Shouldn't the IV be checked?

Answer: No, your arm is not swollen.

Enter the woman's physician. The patient relates her concerns to the MD, who checks the arm, finds it quite hot and swollen, and begins to ask that the IV be removed. Now the nurse begins to ratchet up her displeasure and indicates that there is no physician's order for this, wherein the MD states, "I am the physician!" The MD begins to remove the IV, and the nurse begins shouting that, "There's no doctor's order for that!" The MD ignores her, removes the IV and writes the order. Obviously, the patient is now indicated as a PIA (pain in the ass) by the nursing staff.

Question 3: The patient is thirsty and knows she can only tolerate diluted apple juice and asks for some. "No, you can only have diluted orange juice," she is told even though the patient (and probably the nurse) knows that this will not be tolerated by the patient's stomach. The result is more vomiting.

Question 4: Can I have some ice chips? Nurse: "No, you cannot." Shift change occurs, and an older, more experienced nurse comes on, to whom the patient makes the same request. "Of course you can have ice chips," the nurse replies. "Who said you couldn't?" The patient tells her how it played out earlier, and the second nurse says, "Well, you were dealing with an idiot." She gets her ice chips.

This type of resistant nursing care went on for two days, wherein the patient's MDs and her husband agreed she would best be cared for at home. Discharge on a weekend (not so usual), and off she went.

What was the reason for all of this? Was it inadequate nursing education that led the nurses to toss aside their empathy for a surgery patient? Was it something happening outside the hospital? Did cultural bias or some sense of economic inequality enter into it? All of the aforementioned? Probably.

Healthcare may be a great field and have a sterling reputation for future employment opportunities and stability, but if you can't deal with people with empathy, stay out of it. It is not for those who only want job security and union protection, nor is it for those who are poorly trained and just slipped through their school exams. Chemistry is one thing, people are a totally different matter.

Chapter 61: Size OOO? Thirsting for Quick Profit Designers Tamper with Your Mind

Clothing choices or sizes and many other items you will need to buy are not made by choice but by manipulation of your mind. Designers have found the key to profitability, and you help them.

The saleswoman was pleasant as she asked to help me select a top. "Let me see," she said as she looked me over. "I think you're a 2." Two?

Two? I'd never been anything but a size 8 since I was in grade school, and I'd filled out a bit since then.

My mind was reeling at the thought of selecting anything less than a size 8, and then I began to look at the sizes indicated on the shelves. Who on Earth could be a size 0 or a size 00?

Wouldn't that mean they'd be invisible? Zero indicates the lack of anything, an absence, nothing less than that. I wanted to see a size 0, but none seemed to be walking around. Maybe they were in intensive care at the hospital. Bad joke, I know.

Since the average American woman was a size 14, the design industry has worked diligently to ingrain in women's minds, *You are what we say you are*. And women have bought it in some ersatz belief of petiteness.

In reality, the "average American woman" is no longer size 14; she is sizes 16–18 or 20W. That is a long way from size 0.

Vanity Sizing Enters the World

Attempting to create the illusion of slenderness and help promote those "beach bodies" that women are struggling to maintain, the design world came up with vanity sizing. It is a marketing illusion.

"Today, clothing manufacturers are often using "vanity sizing," the labeling of clothes with sizes smaller than the actual cut of the items. So, those size 34 slacks might really be closer to size 36, and perhaps even bigger."

Finding a size 10 in one store means you'll need a size 8 in another or a size 2 or even a size 000, as I was told. If this isn't sheer nonsense, I don't know what might be categorized that way. There is no uniformity of sizing, and each manufacturer decides how to size their clothing. Is there a difference in the amount of material in the garment? No. Why the change in sizing then?

Psychology is at the center of this sizing mania, and it's all in the service of someone's self-esteem. "Across five studies, we demonstrate that larger sizes result in negative evaluations of clothing and show that these effects are driven by consumers' appearance self-esteem. Importantly, we also find that instead of unilaterally lowering purchase intent as one might assume, larger sizes can actually increase spending, as consumers engage in compensatory consumption to help repair their damaged self-esteem." But wait, something is happening to design, and, again, it's in the service of profitability.

The movement by larger women began a few years ago by some retailers with a prescient view of the future who noted changes. The make-believe Petites were really bigger women, and the plus-size model began to inch into the market.

Vogue began a "Shape" issue "every April to celebrate the beauty and well-being of women's bodies." But despite the publication of new magazines dedicated to fuller figures and major modeling agencies offering models of a certain size, vanity sizing continues.

Pummeling a woman's self-esteem doesn't sound like good business, but it goes along with the diet industry that persists in indoctrinating women to buy more diet systems or foods. Each year 45 million Americans go on a weight-loss program. These are billion-dollar industries, and if they continue to thrive, why would anyone cease their operation?

But research has shown that diets don't work, so once a company offers a diet plan, it's like putting a hamster in a wheel in a cage; they keep on trying.

Despite the evidence, the advertising persists as 30 million people (20 million women and 10 million men) develop eating disorders. Anyone prone to being concerned about weight, and all of us should be, will want to learn how to best control body weight (BMI) and calculate it for health reasons. Vanity also enters into the picture, and that is where the money lies.

An example of dieting is Oprah Winfrey, a billionaire who now owns a 10% share in WW (Weight Watchers). How many diets has she tried, and how successful has she been? Look at Oprah over the years, and the evidence is in front of you.

Even Weight Watchers has carefully tiptoed away from the "weight" in their name, changing it to WW. It's not a weight-control culture or diet program any longer? Then why would they be selling calorie-controlled frozen foods and snacks? Now it's a lifestyle company?

If weight and what you eat are on your mind almost 24 hours a day, when do you have time to be creative or have a life outside dieting? Is dieting the central theme of your life? Don't cults use this technique to keep their devotees in line, constantly reciting or reading specific passages?

And those size 000 designers are right up there cheering you on in your dieting. After all, sample size shoes are about a size 6–7, dress size 2–4, and jeans size 27. To have a 27-inch waist, would a woman have to have a rib removed? The average American woman's waist is now 38 inches.

I suppose to get a size 000 top, a woman would have to be an advocate of the researcher Ancel Keys, who starved men in his study. I once saw a famous singer in a Broadway diner eating a cracker with a glass of water and a lemon slice. She was a skeleton of a person then. Now she is overweight.

Social media and advertising influence eating disorders intended to meet the impossible standards set by designers and corporations. As we've seen before, first create the problem and then provide the solution.

Information on eating disorders can be obtained from the NIMH.

Chapter 62: Skip Your Way to Better Body Conditioning Instead of Running

Running has gained a place in our exercise routine, but there's something even better, and it feels like a return to our childhood.

Scientific research has come to many conclusions, but one may be rather surprising and, in its simplicity, offer us an excellent way to improve both our bodies and our minds—skipping. When was the last time you tried to skip, or how old were you when you regularly skipped along the street? Most people would probably scoff at skipping as just a childhood way to show enjoyment. But it's more than that.

Skipping is now considered one of the simplest equipment-free exercises. In fact, skipping may be more beneficial than jogging or walking. And we know that skipping for adults also engages novelty, which is essential for exercise programs.

As a youngster in elementary school, I marveled at how the girls ran into the jump rope being held by a girl at either end of the long rope. When they played Double Dutch, I was genuinely amazed. Whenever I tried to run into the rope, I failed; when I tried to jump rope, I had difficulty, too.

As a matter of fact, when I related the story to one of my college classes, they found it both amusing and interesting. On the last day of class, they presented me with a simple, inexpensive jump rope. No, I have not managed to conquer my inability to jump rope. I decided to stick to rollerskating and riding my bike. Let me leave it at that.

Childhood is a time to develop specific skills, and skipping and rope jumping can benefit us in the long term. We know now that either jumping rope or skipping on a regular schedule can maintain bone density. Of course, bone density is especially important for women as they age because they will lose this aspect of their skeletal structure and be at greater risk for fractures.

How many women in their 70s and 80s suffer hip fractures, which can have life-threatening consequences? A neighbor of mine recently fell and fractured her hip; she is in her late 80s and lives alone in her apartment. After surgery, she developed an infection, had to be sent for a time to a rehab facility, and now her life has been turned upside down. She has lost her independence to a significant extent. Now, the family must collaborate with her to determine where she will reside and who she will live with. Living alone no longer seems to be a viable option for her.

What Research Indicates

There is very little research available that examines explicitly the effects of skipping without a rope. Most of the research is on rope skipping, a coordinated arm movement and rope use activity that may provide additional benefits in coordination and rhythm. However, the basic movement of jumping is the same in both activities. Therefore, it can be assumed that skipping without a rope may also provide similar physical benefits, such as better cardiovascular fitness, lower body strength, and caloric expenditure.

A single skip merges elements of running with jumping through alternating movements to produce a distinct biomechanical movement. When you skip, you start with one foot, then take a brief flight before stepping down with the other foot and continuing this pattern. Your body requires synchronized movement between your upper and lower body to maintain proper alignment, while your core muscles activate to support this alignment.

The skipping movement produces different effects than jumping rope because it combines side-to-side motions with rotation and opposite-sided movements. The dynamic skipping action activates your body's proprioception system, which generates higher neuromuscular demands than standard workouts.

For example, a study published in 2022 found that an 8-week rope-skipping program improved standing long jump performance in male college students. They also found that there was an improvement in the velocity of the center of gravity at takeoff and landing, which means that there was an improvement in lower body power and coordination. (mdpi.com)

This study is on rope skipping, but the core activity of repetitive jumping is the same for both rope and ropeless skipping. Therefore, it is possible that skipping without a rope can provide similar benefits in terms of lower body strength and power. Men, too, benefit from this type of exercise that can be done anywhere, anytime and without any equipment whatsoever.

Although there is very limited direct research on skipping without a rope, the available research on rope skipping indicates that the main movement involved, jumping, is quite physically beneficial. Thus, skipping without a rope is also likely to offer similar benefits, especially for lower body strength and cardiovascular fitness.

Now that you are acquainted with the benefits of skipping, don't stop yourself if you happen to be outside taking a leisurely walk and decide to incorporate a bit of skipping into it. That would be a great benefit, but one of the things that you must put aside is that it is a "childish" activity. No, it's not.

Skipping is a very good health-promoting activity, and you should do it if you can and if your PCP indicates it's fine for you. Remember, not everyone may have the agility required, and we want everyone to be safe as they exercise.

Chapter 63: Strength Beyond Years: How Exercise Redefines Aging

New research contradicting the myth that aging results in irretrievable muscle loss needs to confront that myth.

Exercise is for everyone, and limiting it to only those under a certain age is irresponsible because it is essential to exercise at any age. We don't need research to tell us this if we look at those walking around us. In a local pharmacy, the woman dispensing medication told me she has a woman who comes in to get her medication, and the woman is 103 years old. According to her pharmacist, she comes alone, walks without a walker, occasionally may have a cane, and is apparently in good health. How did she get there? One truth is evident—regular exercise, and I don't mean the painful kind.

What's more, exercise is just not for your muscles and your strength. I've written on why muscles are involved in mood, and you can go to this article to refresh your memory or read it if you haven't already.

What recent research benefits those over 70? Undoubtedly, we have a great deal more in terms of input in our muscle maintenance than anyone thought when they considered people over 70. The newest research refutes that myth, providing new insights and amazing changes for this group.

But there are specific periods in our lives when certain changes will begin, and with each phase, there will be almost indiscernible changes. However, there are indications that those above 70, who are at greatest risk for instability, balance problems, muscle weakness, and even bone fractures, require our attention. Previously, adequate work was not directed at the potential maintenance and retrieval of muscle strength in this group, and that is where new, exciting research is coming to the fore.

What Are the Groups?

Sarcopenia is the medical term for muscle loss, and it is a normal aging process that affects all humans, although the rate of onset and the severity of the condition are different among individuals. This slowdown in muscle mass, strength, and function has implications for the quality of life and dependence of the elderly. Muscle loss occurs at different ages, and we need to pay attention to enable people to prevent or at least remediate this to some extent.

20s-30s Age Group

In the young adulthood (20s to 30s) age group, muscle mass is at its peak. This age group is likely to have the best muscle strength and function as most people. The body is well equipped to build up and preserve muscle tissue as long as the muscle is used and fed properly. However, even at this young stage, people with sedentary jobs may already experience some muscle atrophy that does not manifest itself clinically. It sets the stage for future deterioration, so appropriate physical activity and diet during these years are a sound investment into future muscle health.

40s Group

Beginning in the 40s, the person begins to show some changes as mentioned above. The literature reviews indicate that muscle mass starts to decline at about 0.5–1% every year after age 30 and the rate increases a little in the 40s. It is also the time when strength reduction is first noticed especially in muscle fibers which control power and speed.

The quadriceps, hamstrings, and calf muscles may start to weaken, especially in people with low levels of physical activity. Most people in this age bracket feel the fatigue and reduced physical endurance when engaging in physical activities.

50s Group

More specific features of muscle atrophy can be observed in the 50s. The rate of loss is higher, currently ranging between 1–2% every year. At this time, the hormonal changes worsen the muscle regeneration. To women menopause reduces the level of estrogen that accelerates muscle loss. Men also have low levels of testosterone that also worsen the muscle tissue.

The abdominal muscles and the lower back muscles, which are the stabilizers, also weaken a lot. Upper body strength, especially in the chest, shoulders, and arms, decreases at a higher rate than before.

60 Group

In the 60s, the loss of muscle is higher and the following rates are observed: 2–3% per year. The consequences of the changes are seen in the everyday life and the person needs help in performing certain actions. The muscles of the lower limb that include the quadriceps, hamstrings and gluteal muscles also weaken greatly.

Many people in this age group will report having problems with stairs, getting up from a chair, or walking for long distances. The hand grip strength is reduced which in turn affects the fine motor skills and the ability to handle objects. The sense of balance is also affected because muscle weakness and neurological changes in proprioception occur.

Over 70 Group

Muscle loss is at its highest in adults over 70, with annual losses of 3–5% if no schedule for slowing or reversing this loss is introduced. This accelerated decline has a major effect on the quality of life and independence. This age group has distinct muscle weakness with well-defined patterns of muscle involvement that have important functional implications

1. The quadriceps, hamstrings and gluteal muscles are the extremity muscles that are affected to a greater degree. This weakness is manifested as:

2. Difficulty in rising from sitting position
3. Slow walking
4. High chances of falling
5. Difficulty in climbing stairs

The ankles are also liable to weaken, and this causes the client to have difficulty with walking and increased chances of falling.

Strengthen these muscle groups by including functional exercises that may involve using body weight, resistance bands, or light weights. Of course, any exercise routine in any age group should always be planned with a certified trainer or someone in a rehabilitation facility specifically to address these needs.

Some of the exercises that can be of great help include standing from a chair, slow walks, sitting leg raises, and ankle exercises to build strength. Exercises in water are an excellent way to work on these muscles with minimum impact on the joints.

Balance is trained very effectively by standing exercises that reduce the base of support step by step. The tandem stance is particularly effective — this is when one stands with one foot in front of the other, heel to toe, to begin with, leaning on a sturdy chair or counter. In the event that stability improves, the support can be reduced to a fingertip touch, then to no support at all.

The single-leg stance is another basic exercise; start by holding a chair and lifting one foot slightly off the floor for 10–15 seconds and then switch to the other side. This exercise directly strengthens the stabilizing muscles around the hips and ankles that are crucial for the prevention of falls.

Weight-shifting exercises are used to develop the dynamic balance. The weight shift is to stand with feet hip-width apart and then slowly shift weight from one foot to the other without moving the feet. Clock reaches expand on these concepts by visualizing standing at the center of a clock face and reaching one foot towards different 'hours' whilst remaining balanced. These movements enhance proprioception, which is the sense of where the different parts of the body are in space, and this sense is often reduced as one gets older.

The good news is that even though you have lost muscle strength, there is still the ability to help your muscles pull back some of that strength and renew your ability to move and continue an active lifestyle. As has been noted by several of the articles, water exercises seem to be one of the best, especially for anyone with arthritic conditions. And please keep in mind that exercise is intimately associated with mood.

Chapter 64: Do Organ Transplants Implant Personal Traits in Recipients?

A few studies have uncovered what may "show" aspects of the donor in those who receive the transplanted organ.

Organ transplants are believed to be the process of implanting an organ from a donor in a new recipient — nothing more. However, several studies focus on the unsettling beliefs or behaviors that recipients reveal relative to the donors. No, it's not something from Mary Shelley's writings or Tim Burton's films, and it is both intriguing and curious, perhaps frightening, at the same time.

The belief has always been that memory resides in the brain, yet we know there may be other types of memory reservoirs that don't remain in the brain but may be in other areas of our bodies, organs, or anywhere. Just because we haven't discovered all of them doesn't mean they don't exist.

We are now in an era of discovery, probably unlike any other era aside from the time when Leonardo da Vinci was doing dissections and anatomic drawings in his studio. New observations are pushing us into these areas of the unknown; some are stunning, and one area is heart transplants.

Overall, these findings support the idea that heart transplant patients experience "exosome memory transfer." There is evidence to support the idea that at least some of our memories are stored in the heart and move around in the blood pathways over time. This idea simplifies at least some parts of how the heart works when remembering things. Memories are mostly made in the brain, but it's not the only place.

Exosomes move memory from the cells to the heart and back again. This changes all the time, throughout a person's life. The nerve paths do not play a role at all or very little. Still, this does not mean that memories do not also form in the heart. This idea is not completely ruled out, either. Exosome memory transfer could be one reason people with heart transplants change who they are.

In 2020, just under 8200 heart transplants were done worldwide; in 2021, more than 144,000 organs were transferred. Transplantation surgery can have big effects on a person's mental health, and some patients worry that they will take on the personality traits of their donor.

Studies examining heart donation recipients have found that their personalities change after getting a new organ. Some of them even started to exhibit traits that were present in their donors. Reports like this have been found in both medical and non-medical journals. Did they receive information on their donors and unconsciously incorporate some traits and believe it was because the heart carried these traits with it?

A study in Canada looked at 27 teenage heart transplant recipients and found that many of them had trouble integrating their ideas of "self" and "other" (i.e., their donated organ). Some of them also had thoughts or questions about possibly taking on the traits of their donor through their donor's heart. However, the frequency of mental changes remained unspecified.

People who received kidney, liver, or other organs also said their emotions, sense of smell, and food preferences changed after the transplant. However, these changes were generally temporary and not as strong as the changes seen in people who received hearts

Reports of mental changes and memories of past events are becoming more prevalent. One woman who had a heart and lung transplant said that after her surgery, she noticed changes in her habits, views, and tastes. She had strange cravings for foods she used to hate. For example, she was a dancer and director who cared about her health, but as soon as she got out of the hospital, she had to go to Kentucky Fried Chicken and order chicken nuggets, which she never did.

Now, it made her feel better to wear cool colors instead of the bright reds and oranges she used to like. She began to behave differently, adopting mannerisms and attitudes reminiscent of the donor. In a strange twist, Kentucky Fried Chicken nuggets that had not been eaten were found in the jacket of the young male giver who had been killed.

Anyone interested in reading more on the subject might want to read "*The Heart's Code*," which details findings related to heart transplants and changes recipients have experienced.

Some patients are afraid that their personalities might change after receiving an organ transplant. Recommendations are that this is something that should be talked about with potential transplant recipients before they go through with the surgery, as it might make them less hesitant and more likely to follow through with their post-transplant treatment. Heart transplant recipients (91.3%) and other organ transplant patients (87.5% of participants) said they had changed somehow. These results show that personality changes are common after any organ donation, though this may again be due to selection bias.

As the results of many studies over the past 50 years have indicated, there are more memory stories in places we never considered. Stored memories may reside in organs used for transplant and may result in recipients experiencing changes no one had ever expected.

Chapter 65: Before Summer: Life Lesson Children Must Learn—To Swim, But How Many Do?

Swimming isn't simply good exercise or fun with family and friends; it can be the one thing that saves a child's life.

The Centers for Disease Control and Prevention say that ten people die every day in the U.S. from unintentional drowning, including 1 in 5 children 14 or younger. Drowning is the second most common cause of unintentional injury death for children and the fifth most common cause of unintentional injury death for people of all ages. For every child who drowns and dies, five others go to the emergency room with submersion injuries that do not result in death.

But drowning isn't limited to small children or deaths in the bathtub. Teenagers may be too sure of their swimming skills and are more likely to swim while drunk, which greatly increases their risk. Children of color, especially African American teens, are particularly vulnerable to this risk.

Black kids between the ages of 5 and 14 are 2.6 times more likely to die than white kids of the same age. This is because Black families have not had much experience with public pools and other water activities over the years because they have been shut out of them.

Overall, the number of drowning deaths has gone down, but there are still differences between racial and ethnic groups. To help close these gaps, community-based interventions could be used to teach disproportionately affected racial and ethnic groups basic swimming and water safety skills. From 2005 to 2019, the difference in the number of non-Hispanic Black and White people who drowned grew. From 1999 to 2019, 81,947 people died in the United States by drowning accidentally.

While overall drowning death rates have gone down, there are still differences between racial and ethnic groups. Implementing and evaluating community-based interventions, such as those that teach racial and ethnic groups fundamental swimming and water safety skills, could help to reduce these differences.

The difference in the number of drownings of Black and white males in Florida went down from 1970 to 1990. By 2005, the overall age-adjusted drowning rate had leveled off. The decrease was most noticeable for people ages 10 to 34 and 35 to 64. Even though the gap has gone down quite a bit, there is still a racial difference in drownings among those ages 10 to 34.

In terms of children, there are new guidelines from the American Academy of Pediatrics that explain how to keep kids safe at all stages of their lives. For example, new parents should be extra careful during bath time and make sure that all buckets and wading pools are empty right away. All kids should learn to swim, and kids and teens should wear life jackets when they are near open bodies of water. Teens can also learn CPR and other water safety skills. Research has shown that children as young as 1 can benefit from swimming classes, and these lessons may also lower the number of kids who drown.

Any area near open bodies of water, be they oceans, lakes, rivers, or streams, is an opportunity for water-related drowning deaths. But how many cities, especially in areas where those with lower incomes live, offer any type of water safety or swimming programs? One place is New York City.

New York City officials say that the free swim lessons program helps about 30,000 people a year and costs $2.5 million a year. If you think that sounds like a lot of people participating, consider that in the city there are almost a million kids in public schools, and the budget is $101 billion a year. Are there enough kids learning to swim in these programs that appear to have paltry funding for their existence?

In addition, consider that New York City has enormous stretches of beaches where teenagers go to escape the seasonal heat waves. How many deaths occur at those beaches because the kids can't swim or aren't strong swimmers and may go to beaches unprotected by life-guards?

The National Weather Service provides a map indicating **Surf Zone Fatalities** with preliminary data and links to other sources of information on surf-related fatalities. In 2023, the majority of incidents occurred along the Atlantic Ocean's beaches. They indicate, however, that the data are approximations.

Consider some of the water-related facts about the New York/New Jersey area around New York City and its five boroughs. The New York-New Jersey Harbor Estuary has over 770 miles of shoreline with navigable waterways. It is one of the biggest natural harbors in the world.

How many kids jump into those waters each year to frolic in their cool, increasingly cleaner waters? How many are found dead along some of its rocky outcroppings each year? How many don't know about the undertow or riptides or how swiftly and strongly the rivers' channels' tides can change? The Hudson River is referred to as a *drowned river* because the Atlantic sends surges of its saltwater up the Hudson Canyon in the river when the tides change.

Programs that teach anyone to swim at any age are essentially life-saving programs, just as CPR programs are, and we need more of them.

Chapter 66: Lying and the Eagerly Agreeable Dishonest Brain

Habitual lying becomes easier because brain structures make it so. Once again this trait is being exposed in politics and our culture.

Every government is run by liars, and nothing they say should be believed. — I. F. Stone

Our brains, those boneless, three-pound, jelly-like, wrinkled organs with billions of connections all running simultaneously, are servants that eagerly await our wishes (our "code," if you will). Sitting up there in its bony catacomb are two small structures that incorporate a host of biological commands and emotions, some good and some designed to deceive: the amygdalae.

Part of our most primitive pathways in the brain, the amygdalae do a job related to basic emotions and drives. However, they also act as if they are actively engaged in deep learning to enhance their ability to react appropriately. It is here that we train these structures to help us lie and to deceive polygraph machines.

I'll never forget the first time I saw a human brain, actually a collection of human brains, floating freely in large glass containers in a hospital morgue collection. The attendant, who was intent on showing me as much as I could bear, pointed out that human brains are not grey but pinkish when first removed from the skull. It is the formaldehyde in which they are preserved that turns them a light shade of gray.

I wasn't that interested in brains at the time, and he proceeded to show me a collection of disfigured aortas from young men who had died in recent wars. Then we walked over to the refrigerators, and he opened one of the small doors, sliding out the rack as he did.

Thank God he didn't pick one that had a body on it, or I would have run out of that room. Afterward, I would smell of formaldehyde for hours; it had permeated my clothing. Now, I would've been more interested in the brains.

Learning to Feel Better About Lying

Lying doesn't occur without effort. We decide to plan how we will lie (the mode here), and then we put the lie into action. During this process, our brain shifts into a lie mode where biological processes such as changes in respiration, heart rate, and blood pressure all kick in. Although these are natural biological responses, research indicates that we can enhance our brain's activity by practicing deception sufficiently. As in so much else, practice, practice, practice doesn't make perfect, but much more effortless.

As shown by brain studies using small fMRI scanning, the amygdala responds in one way when a person initially attempts to deceive but diminishes this response as the person continues to practice lying. In other words, the amygdala is waiting to be trained to engage in less action in habitual liars.

Over time, there is less and less of this biological reaction to lying. Therefore, the response to dishonesty is perceived as a normal part of functioning in this individual.

Whatever the current moral code might be, these dishonest and lying individuals will manage to be self-protective from any sense of discomfort as they continue with this behavior. In fact, in addition to the amygdala, another portion of our brain, the prefrontal cortex, where judgments are made, also plays a role in what has been known as the "Pinocchio Syndrome."

Does Lying Have a Place in Society?

We know that in certain social situations, telling the absolute, unvarnished truth may be both unacceptable and, in some ways, problematic. Therefore, we engage, probably regularly, in what we term "little white lies." Of course, this is a way of soothing our conscience and telling ourselves that this behavior is okay but necessary to survive in our culture.

Initially, children are not adept at lying and must learn the two rules to be applied; rule one is that they can recognize and understand social rules and consequences for transgression. The other is the ability to assess and imagine the thoughts of the person being lied to. This ability will continue to develop with the child's cognitive skills. For some children, lying may also be a matter of a life-and-death approach in their particular situation.

It takes time, however, to become skilled. A 2015 study with more than 1,000 participants looked at lying in volunteers in the Netherlands aged six to 77. Children, the analysis found, initially have difficulty formulating believable lies, but proficiency improves with age. Young adults between 18 and 29 do it best. After about the age of 45, we begin to lose this ability.

Not only must the liar learn to lie effectively, but they must also learn to inhibit telling the truth and percolating into their lies' scenarios. The liar must work at lying and effectively remember the lie's facts so that they will not trip themselves up when deceiving another.

Our results also suggest that dishonesty escalation is contingent on the motivation for the dishonest act. The amygdala's response to dishonesty over time and the increase in dishonesty were best explained by whether it was self-serving. When participants were dishonest for the benefit of someone else, dishonesty at a constant rate was observed. This is consistent with the suggestion that the motivation for acting dishonestly contributes to its affective assessment, such that when a person engages in dishonesty purely for the benefit of another, it may be perceived as morally acceptable. Thus, the simple act of repeated dishonesty is not enough for escalation to take place, but a self-interest motive needs to be present.

Lying and Its Purpose

It would seem from the results of these studies by Garrett et al. (2016) that altruism and self-interest also play a role in the utility of lying. Therefore, lying can be seen as a necessary evil when it is used for the good of others.

An example is in a prisoner-of-war camp during World War II, where the Nazis asked any Jew in a line to step forward. A Catholic priest stepped forward to save a Jew. He became known as the Saint of Auschwitz.

The Rev. Maksymilian Kolbe, the Polish priest who volunteered in Auschwitz to die in another man's stead, was proclaimed a saint of the Roman Catholic Church today.

The man whose life the priest saved, Franciszek Gajowniczek, lived to the age of 94 and witnessed the priest's courage.

There have also been other instances where people have been willing to sacrifice their life for the life of another, but that does not diminish the significance of the moral courage shown by any of them.

The question of lying remains one of purpose and intent. Those who lie purposefully to deceive others for self-interest are not seen as candidates for rehabilitation from lying. It just becomes too easy for them and is an ingrained part of their personality.

For the rest of us, lying will remain a part of our culture since it does have a place not necessarily in self-protective areas but in protecting others. However, if we are not habitual liars, is there a cost associated with lying? The answer is probably dependent on the outcome of the lie.

Chapter Sixty-Seven

Chapter 67: Bye, Bye Miss American Pie and All That

The pop hit may not be something with which you are familiar, but today it seems an apt lament to all that is going, going, gone in this world that is obsessed with technology and total ignorance of how to truly interact with people. For sure, we are losing our people skills, and I suppose it really came home when I watched the film "**Gone Girl**" last night.

The film, which I highly recommend, is almost an ode to the fake veneer of acceptable sociability that seems so evident today. Forget about constantly looking over your shoulder when greeting someone. Scanning the room has always been there and will always be in a world that has too many tinges of narcissism and self-promotion. There is a persistent campaign to marginalize the good guys and those who are authentic. Are we getting ready for a campaign to return to the earth and create truly honest, caring relationships? Time will tell.

The theme popped up, too, as I read articles on the late Gov. Mario Cuomo of New York. A man of the people who came from a poor area of Queens, didn't speak English for his first years, went to what is termed a "blue collar" law school, and rose to be an orator's orator. He was on the verge of running for president and receiving an appointment to the US Supreme Court, but he requested the removal of his name. What a justice he would have made. We can only imagine the arguments and briefs he would have written and how he would have championed the little people. What a loss, but he had his reasons, and some of them, I'm sure, were highly private.

Cuomo, you see, was a man who believed in doing what he set out to do and felt he had more of an obligation to the people of New York who elected him and didn't want to leave until he had completed his work. How many people do you know who would have refused such an incredible appointment? It's lifetime. In legal terms, you hold the ultimate authority over the law of the land. Incredible, but he did turn it down.

A new Congress begins this week, and already there are rumblings about what the newly elected and incredibly green representatives will try to push on the American people. Congress is no longer representative of the people. Examine the sources of their campaign funds to quickly understand the implications of upcoming legislative initiatives. One, of course, will be to push through the Keystone Pipeline as a job creator. The deal is just to set up the transport of Canadian oil through the US to a Gulf of Mexico port for export. Jobs? Hardly. Want a quick education on this? Watch whatever you can find that has been prepared by **Bill Moyers**, one of the truly fine journalists still left, who is leaving his TV program.

Moyers, as you may not know, started out as a Baptist minister, and he has maintained a straight-arrow approach to every topic of vital interest to the American people. His voice, which is sorely needed right now, will no longer be heard on PBS, and that is not a shame. It is a deficit from which we may never return to honesty in journalism free from fear of job loss or corporate action. Does that sound familiar? Whoever owns the media holds sway over our entire country and much of how the people think.

The opiate of the people isn't religion; it is deficient media that burps forth inconsequential articles and programs that serve only to put American intellectualism into a deeper stupor. "Why teach kids to write?" asks one article. Write? We shouldn't teach children to write? Why give them books that tax their ability to reason? Toss out the Socratic method and bring on "Mob Wives," and they'll be satisfied. Infantilize the entire TV audience and do it, of course, via all media devices as well, and you will have won a battle that no one ever suspected was being fought.

Wealthy people in China are paying thousands of dollars to learn how to attend an elegant dinner party and even more for a Birkin bag. They want to know how to hold their utensils, which fork to use, and what to do with their napkins after eating. But what they don't see is the truly incongruous action on their part displayed by their continuous use of cell phones and texting during the meal. Isn't that considered rude behavior? Champagne flutes and red wine balloons are fine to know about, but do they make for cultured persons? A buffoon can pick up the proper fork, but he's still a buffoon. So, out the window with culture and bring on the Tom Joneses of the 21st century. Bawdy behavior and worshiping at the altar of Adephagia may be fashionable again if we can believe what we've seen in "**The Wolf of Wall Street.**" Is Gordon Gekko the man we should revere and kneel down before?

So, you can see that films really do reveal a lot, don't they? As I watch the film this evening, I'll be looking not just for the storyline but for what it says about our culture. Would anyone have made "**It's a Good Life**" this year? Don't know. Maybe there is another George Bailey out there, and he's waiting to make his entrance on the stage. Watch for him.

Chapter 68: College Needs Training in Responsibility or Penalties for Fraud?

The ugly scandal at one American university with a stellar record for athletic achievement has bubbled out of its well-hidden ivory tower encampment, and the stench is awful. Twenty years or more in the making and active participation in promoting educational fraud, and one of their management teams had little believable substance to offer.

It seems, she said, "We have to do a better job of training for responsibility." Can you buy this? Training for responsibility—just what does that mean in anything other than PRspeak? Don't people come to higher education settings with that programmed into their DNA by years of acting responsibly? I'm talking about administrators, not students, here. What wonderful role models they are. They not only enable this academic fraud, but they also seem to have promoted it, though we don't have all the details.

What we do know is more than disturbing. Wouldn't you want to, if you were so inclined, get a degree without ever having to take a course with anything but one paper to write? And, of course, you could always buy a paper or write it in whatever incoherent drivel you wished, and you'd get a more-than-generous grade to pass. No, you wouldn't. What's more, it seems the courses were myths that really didn't exist on anything but some administrator's computer. Wouldn't you agree that such conduct is out-and-out theft of a certain type? Theft of academic promise, theft of future security, and deception of the most egregious type are all involved here.

The administration, either from one department or possibly more, handled everything for the athletes. How dishonorable can they be, and how did they think they were benefiting the athletes? Obviously, they were only benefiting the school's athletics program and keeping the funds flowing from thrilled alumni. Are the alumni still satisfied, and will the athletes eventually benefit from their degrees?

Okay, you wouldn't do this because you actually believe that going to college means you agree to stick to the honor code, and you really want to learn something. College isn't just something to keep you in your parents' home or in a cushy lifestyle out of the dog-eat-dog job world.

The coaches claim that they were totally unaware of the deception. I can't buy that one either if the coaches have functioning neurons in their noodles. They do plan incredibly accurate and winning plays for their teams, don't they? Don't they also demand intense practice, workouts and whatever will benefit the sport in which they participate? How can the athletes get these grades if they spend most of their time in sports activities? No, it doesn't wash.

Are we now going to hear the moans of the upper levels of the school, where they also knew all of this was too good to be true? Whose head/s will roll here? One chairman had already left before the full impact of the deception hit the media. Should he have legal charges against him? Should the parents of athletes have the right to sue for theft of services or some other legal action? Did the athletes get an education, or were they just pawns in all of this? No one is going to accept the jocks as pawns, either, I believe. They fully knew what they were doing, and they knew it wasn't kosher, but they continued because it had been so well run that being caught didn't seem to be an option.

It's like something out of the TV series "Breaking Bad." Slowly the scheme rolls forward and with each success, the darker side of the personalities begins to take over and out the door go ethics, honor and reputation. We've seen it before, and we'll see it again. Does money play such a commanding role in higher education that considerations of academic honesty must be pushed aside?

Certainly the fall of Joe Paterno at Penn State cast a glaring and very unflattering light on college athletics. Paterno denied he knew anything about the sex scandal that was about to unseat him and rattle the school to its very core. I'm not saying he did anything apart from tend to football. But it seems he should have also been attending to other things that needed immediate intervention. Kids were being sexually abused by someone to whom he gave free rein in the lockers, shower rooms and other areas of his domain.

Sports are supposed to instill a spirit of cooperation in groups and leadership skills that will last a lifetime. At least that's what we psychologists have always thought, and it's one of the reasons people supported the initiatives to get equal funds for women's college sports activities. But sports are one aspect of personality development, and you can't shove your principles under the proverbial basket and leave them behind as you go about promoting sports at all costs.

Dishonor has been brought on the school, and careers may have been ruined. I wonder how many will take early retirement and leave the poorly served athletes swinging in the wind.

Chapter 69: Two Weeks in Bell Labs: A snippet of an ordeal

A sk any research scientist worth their salt where the premier research facility existed in the past 100 years or so, and they'll probably say Bell Labs. The arcane facility was originally located on the West Side of lower Manhattan. It was the percolator for ingenious patents, wildly creative stabs at advancing the science of technology, and the brainchild of Thomas Edison. And it was a place where anyone who got a job was going to be there for life.

Researchers had unbelievable freedom to follow their curiosity without being hampered by timelines or budgets. It was like falling into nirvana, and it must have been the equivalent of an intellectual playpen for adults. Okay, too many comparisons and stretching to make the point here. If you want to read all about it, get a copy of *"Bell Labs: Life in the Crown Jewel"* by Narain Gehani.

But while the boys were romping around the huge facility and creating everything from the transistor to every conceivable gadget in technology, there was another force working to support them—the unseen girls in the steno pool. The hope of any of these young women was that a secretary would either retire or die because that was the only path to getting out of the pool.

There were two distinct worlds, and I was in the one that worked in anonymity and under strict rules. Today, you might see it as an *"Upstairs, Downstairs"* scenario, only we had less freedom. So, while the golden-haired men joked and walked around (encouraged in order to stimulate creativity), we remained chained invisibly to our Remingtons.

No laughter here or interesting banter. There wasn't a word spoken between even those sitting all day side-by-side. Should a comment be necessary, it was whispered with all the intended collusion of those attempting a prison break. It *was a prison* without bars where they used all the intimidating tactics found in such an institution. Silence swept over the place except for the striking of metal keys on thick packets of paper. Not a whimper, not a cough, nothing. Only human silence.

Until either of the two occasions of retirement or death occurred, you were not exactly chained to your electric typewriter, but you might as well have been. It was worse than boot camp, and you hadn't done anything wrong, and you didn't know how long it would last.

Sounds like Purgatory, doesn't it? But even in Purgatory, you knew the length of your sentence. You were supposed to have attained a dream job of importance after an incredible series of psychological and skill tests and the most complete medical exam ever, but it sure didn't seem like anything more than drudgery.

Let me provide a mental picture of what I experienced for the brief time I toiled at their facility on West Street. For one thing, I was assigned a typewriter set up at something like a lunch table in a prison. It was a row of typewriters bolted to desks that ran horizontally across the room. There must have been 6 of us in a row and at least 6 rows. A straight-back chair and a kit of absolutely essential tools were at each desk. The kit included a razor blade, a stick of white chalk, an exceptionally sharp #2 pencil, a pencil sharpener bolted to the desk, one typewriter cover, and a typewriter eraser. Next to each station was a small wastepaper basket, which served a different purpose than you might imagine.

The rest of the world may casually look at a wastepaper basket as an object meant only to catch the drek we choose to toss into it. It is the recipient of our thrown-away ideas, communications from others, torn envelopes, empty or dry pens, and all manner of stuff we no longer find useful.

At Bell Labs, this basket gained a new level of special prominence, and its ultimate goal was not to be emptied into a large bin but to end up first at the desk of the supervisor in charge of the pool. Each keystroke and piece of paper would be carefully calculated to maintain a running assessment of each girl's productivity for every day. Yes, it was a productivity measure. None of us wanted anything to end up in that basket, and that increased our stress.

Stacked on the left-hand side of each typewriter was something called a "setup." Setups came to us from a basement facility where older women, the setup girls, toiled each day. You never saw them except for the times you may have bumped into them as you and everyone else crowded the stairs leading into the facility in the morning and had your security badge examined.

Once inside the building, the setup girls would proceed to their lockers in the basement, where they put on their pocketed aprons and immediately got to work. I have no idea what their daily quota was, but they too must have been under the gun to keep production up. And do you know that most of these "girls" got their jobs via a recommendation from either a family member who worked at the facility or a friend who did? It was incredibly incestuous but a bit better than when they wouldn't hire the Irish or Catholics, so I've been told.

These "girls" (most in their 50s) carefully produced each packet with one sheet of #20 bond paper on top, then six sheets of onion skin paper, each separated with one sheet of carbon paper, all held together with one paper clip. Some of the sheets were of different colors, but I can't remember them now. Thank God for some small favors. *Setups* were the stuff of life in the pool, and everything we typed was on a setup.

When we began typing from either our steno notes (BTW, we spent two weeks in daily classes learning technological steno brief forms) or items given to us, it became a struggle with the clunky electric typewriter, our too-eager hands and stuck keys. When an error was found, that meant we had to go through the dogged process of correcting that all-too-important first page of bond paper and then, one by one, through all those onion skin pages.

How did we do it? First you put a piece of paper behind all those carbon sheets. Next you took your razor blade and, using only the sharp corner, you carefully dug or scratched out the errant letter and delicately used your chalk to fill in the space. It all had to be very proficiently performed to avoid making a hole or scarring the paper. Once that met your visual inspection, you proceeded to go through the onion skin sheets with your eraser to remove any of the carbon on them.

The end of the process was to remove the slips of paper, restrike the key and inspect the bond to be sure it was as nearly perfect as you could make it. If it wasn't dark enough because of the chalk, you had your trusty pencil to fill in any spaces that needed it. Yes, that's what the pencil was for: darkening letters. And let's not forget that in this process the bond paper might slip a bit. When that happened, you had to carefully realign it to ensure an accurate restrike on the spot just prepared. Miss your mark, and you might end up with a worthless effort that had to be repeated with a fresh setup, and your error score was sure to act against you in that wastebasket count.

But, wait, when did we ever get a break, and how did that play out in this pool of young women? Seated at the back of the room, on a slightly elevated platform, was the supervisor, who observed our backs and typewriters with all the care of a raptor watching game. Stopping for any reason was cause for immediate action and a stern look; a brief question and a wildly beating heart were all part of it. Her heart never beat wildly, and I suspect she had ice water running through her veins. She was a company woman holding fast to her appointed task to keep these girls working feverishly. Does that sound like Gehani's vision of the Bell Labs he worked in? Not a chance.

Three times a day a bell rings. It was much like the school bells in high school, which signaled a change of classes. This meant that all of us would stop our work and proceed to the empty cafeteria, where we'd have a 15-minute coffee break. There was little time for anything but a cup of coffee and a pastry (very reasonably priced or free as I recall) and then back to the pool with a brief stop at the ladies room. No make-up fixes or hair brushing.

The next bell meant lunch and you'd go to stand in line at the serving tables of hot meals, salads and desserts. Then you'd eat and, if you wanted, go into a very large room that had massive leather couches and overstuffed chairs. It was here that you'd see the researchers smoking or chatting with each other. Pool girls didn't mix with them because they were above our social station in this company. Some researchers snoozed, and others read newspapers. The pool girls just sat quietly.

Back to the desk until your next break at 3PM and then, at 5PM exactly, you'd cover your typewriter, straighten your desk and go home.

There was, of course, a pecking order even in the pool. Those young women who had been there longest were the favored few and were called upon by the most experienced researchers to come for dictation. I recall one who was hoping that she was getting very near to a promotion to secretary because one secretary was about to retire.

I never knew if she got the long-anticipated promotion because I left after two weeks. It was not what I had signed on for, and I didn't want to endure the drudgery of this type of existence. After all, I had been the only kid in 5th grade in grammar school who refused to sign the petition to the town's mayor that I would be a good child. Good child? I didn't need to sign anything to agree to that. I *was* a good child. Pressure from the nun with the statement that, *"You are the only child who hasn't signed this,"* didn't work, and I held out. The petition went to the mayor without my signature. The gutsy kid was now up against Ma Bell's production percolator.

I wasn't the first to leave. A young woman, known as Miss Brown, had caught the eye of the supervisor, who wasn't keen on her work or her attitude, either. She did have a disturbing habit of asking questions that made the supervisor uncomfortable, and her fate was sealed.

When I decided to tender my two weeks notice of resignation, I was sent for an exit interview. Naive as I was, I thought what I said was confidential between me and the personnel woman. Wrong. By the time I got back to the pool, the supervisor had blood in her eye and began to berate me for my comments. It was truly unpleasant and a betrayal that I had never expected.

They asked for my security badge, made sure I cleaned out my locker, and I was on my way out on that day, which was a Friday. Two weeks notice wasn't necessary for them. It was out immediately lest I poison the others in the pool with this idea of independence.

Oh, did I forget to mention how we were paid? There was no time to cash a check, so a money cart came around to the pool, and each woman received a small brown envelope with her pay in cash in it. This was tendered to you after you signed your check and gave it to the woman with the cart. Containment was the watchword of the day at Bell Labs. Imagine what would happen if they allowed these girls to leave the building to cash their checks. It was unthinkable. I have no idea how the engineer researchers were paid or if they had this liberty of leaving the building. I would suspect they did.

Yes, there was life after Bell Labs, and it was a great deal better than it would have been had I stayed and, who knows, gone to secretarial heaven in the building.

Chapter 70: Where Should We Be Treating Mental Illness?

C hristmastime is the season to be jolly and to shop for presents, stuff ourselves with too much food, and dream of an America where everyone is out caroling nightly. This is the America we'd like to imagine exists in our country because it's comforting, and we do so need comfort right now. Despite our fervent wishes, there's another, very real, upsetting specter here. No, it's not the Ghost of Christmas Past, but the condition of the incarcerated.

The mentally ill are becoming an inordinate burden to communities in the US as ever more persons with these illnesses are arrested and placed in jails and sent on to prisons. Of course, they also add to the bottom line of corporations that manage prisons, and we need to consider this, too. A huge incentive exists here, and we've seen examples of corrupt judges working at odds with the law.

However, the question in your mind might revolve around how this sorry state of affairs has materialized. Are mentally ill persons more likely to be criminals? Certainly, urban myths swirl around the image of the mentally deranged person wielding a brick or a hatchet and attacking innocent people on the street. The brutal murder of a New York City Central Park West psychologist remains in my mind. Details of the case can only lead to a conclusion of severe mental illness unchecked.

This particular image of the crazed person appears to be popping up more often and even in places like China, too, where schoolchildren have been the victims of men with hatchets and knives lashing out and slaughtering them in their classrooms. So, the myth grows and it would appear it's not confined to the United States. But is it truly grounded in fact, or are isolated instances being exploited for inordinate media attention? And, in the end, who will suffer because of this injustice? My answer would be that everyone suffers when we fail to appropriately attend to the ills of a society.

Working in mental health for three decades, I've seen how the current flood of the mentally ill population is beginning to swell prison populations. Several things add to the mix, not the least of which are crimes committed by persons with mental illness who have received little or no treatment or who have refused to continue their treatment.

The mentally ill were poorly served by the deinstitutionalization plans to empty psychiatric hospitals in the early 1970s. The plans were ill-formed with incredibly inept follow-through, and the scoundrels came in to scoop up the bewildered patients.

Those persons who fell through the cracks of an overburdened, poorly supported and managed social structure, with a constantly revolving cadre of inexperienced, green counselors, roam free, sleep on the streets and mingle among shoppers at malls where they seek warmth in winter and coolness in summer. The result of the latter has been architectural change where seating areas have been removed, much like spikes are installed on window ledges to discourage roosting birds. No seats = no homeless hanging around. And the mentally ill are most certainly homeless. Shelters are places of violence to be avoided.

Add to this swelling population the fact that many prisoners are now in their senescence and require not prison but nursing home care. Are nursing home prisoners to become a new cash cow for a burgeoning industry aimed at our seniors? Who is offering Disneyesque plans for them?

One of our major cities, Los Angeles, California, is facing a major mentally ill inmate problem in its jail. Should they spend $1.7B to build a new jail, or is there another solution to housing and helping the mentally ill? No easy solutions for LA or anywhere else.

Mental health professionals have led us to believe that patients can be managed in the community and that's where they belong. No one would disagree that, if there were truly what had been initially intended, it would be more acceptable than prisons where solitary confinement is often the management method. But the devil is in the details. The mentally ill are just one more opportunity for too many interests and even the well-meaning professionals are overwhelmed by the politics, the financial aspects and the commitment of communities.

Families are fiercely committed, but even they are no match for the forces that push for containment in prisons and supervised housing where staff leave at 6PM or earlier. Oh, yes, the mental health centers promise adequate supervision, but do they truly provide it, and are they really up to the task? I think not.

The holidays are not a very happy time for too many people with mental illness.